# BEYOND LEADERSHIP TO DESTINY— JACOB'S LIFETIME JOURNEY WITH GOD

## Spiritual Formation for Third Millennium Leaders

By Charles Haley

xulon PRESS

To Jo Ann, who has shared the long journey which led me to Jacob's epic story

To my parents, who devoted themselves to their two sons

To our family of twenty—a source of loving support, profound privilege and celebration that runs deep

And in all . . . *to God be the glory*

# TABLE OF CONTENTS

# FIRST WORDS –
# WHY JACOB? WHY YOU?

*Only as far as I look, can I see.*
*Only as much as I dream, can I be.*
*Inside everyone is a champion . . .*
*Seek, and ye shall find him*

*Daily Herald*

*In the coming world, they will not ask me: "Why were you*
*not Moses?"*
*They will ask me: "Why were you not Zusya?"*

*Rabbi Zusya-Martin Buber*

A t 1:17 a.m. 1853 B.C. one of the important events in
human history happened to a lumpy figure lying
among the stones in desert darkness. It was so powerful that
3,829 years and thirteen hours later I was able to take a
transforming principle from this man's life and shatter the
defenses of a former aerospace executive who had lost hope
in life. He now faced years of maximum-security confine-
ment in a federal penitentiary. I had the same principle in
mind when I met with a former state governor who was also

about to spend a few months in a penitentiary. While the time notations above are, of course, only guesses, the stories are true and point to the powerful implications of Jacob's life for leaders today.

I have shared insights from Jacob's life with many others because his story has profoundly shaped my life. Jacob's journey has somehow become my own as I have seen my life story in his. "What would you say if you were to meet Jacob?" someone might ask. I don't think I would say anything, since what I know that I know would only be trivialized by my words. A long period of silence would be the only way I could possibly begin interaction with him.

**Why Jacob?**

Our first question is *WHY* we should invest a small slice of life in sharing Jacob's epic journey. Is it so compelling that we can't afford to miss the opportunity and can expect some lifelong change that is really important?

For the past century Jacob has been the *most neglected, controversial and least understood* of any major Bible character, particularly among evangelicals. Some highly esteemed Christian leaders have written books and preached sermons that fail to hit the mark, since they focus on negatives and miss critical positives from Jacob's life. When I asked one of our sons who was attending a Christian grammar school what he thought of Jacob, he said, "He is a sneakweed!" He was getting the message!

When Joseph H. Cohn saw this trend in the 1940s, he wrote somewhat defensively:

Can you find one word of condemnation of Jacob anywhere in the Bible? We have presented this question to many traducers of Jacob's character, and soon discovered that these character assassins became bewildered. . .and finally were compelled to admit

with confusion that not a syllable of condemnation of
Jacob is to be found anywhere in the Word of God!

In spite of this misunderstanding, my book is *not an
apologetic for Jacob's life*, even though it may become a
means of reframing Jacob's life for third-millennium leaders and Bible interpreters. It is not a study of his place in
history, even though it is incredible that one man's life spans
exactly one-half of the fifty chapters of Genesis when this
book quickly scans generations, races, nations, and divisions of mankind against the backdrop of the origins of the
human race, the world and the universe.

Every Jewish person traces his or her lineage to one of
Jacob's twelve sons. God's plan for the world, the authoring
of the Bible, and the coming of Jesus Christ all go directly
back to Jacob and his twelve sons.

Because his names, Jacob and Israel, are used to identify
the Nation, they are referred to about ten times more than
Abraham's and more than twice that of David's. He is the
only character in the Bible whose life is recorded prenatally
all the way through to the moment of his death. Yet, even
these facts do not bring us to the primary reason we share
Jacob's life journey.

My reason for writing is that *Jacob's life is a model of
spiritual and life formation from womb to tomb* for people
who are serious about their life journey. It's the story of God's
interaction and intervention with one man and his response
over the course of his life. We can watch the progression,
development and the eventual product of this wonderful
process in such a personal way that we can make the transition to our own lives. We see what a journey with God looks
like, the way in which spiritual formation happens, and how a
person can live into his or her destiny.

Jacob's life relates so clearly to the venerable tradition
of *pilgrimage*–a transformative journey to a sacred center

full of hardships, darkness, and peril (Phil Cosineau). Parker Palmer once said, "Before we come to that center, full of light, we must travel in the dark." Jacob's life trek is a *pilgrimage roadmap* for leaders today who are journeying with God. From his perspective, Dwight Judy writes:

> Jacob stands at a profound point in Western culture. Jacob is given the name Israel, because he strove with God and man and prevailed. I want to suggest that this image of striving with and against reality, striving to create one's own world in the face of enormous odds, is a hallmark of the Western male soul. . . . We find in Jacob several of the tasks that each man must journey for himself. We find the task of leaving home, taking blessing with us. We find the task of braving the wilderness alone. We find the task of finding the mature love of a woman. We find the task of struggling with the older masculine, as Jacob struggles for what is rightfully his from Laban. We find the task of making one's own creative contribution to culture. We find the task of making peace with God . . . . In general, Jacob's tasks outline the tasks of mature manhood. (p. 7).

While your experiences are much different than Jacob's, the principles and plan of God for a life are timeless. In some ways, Jacob's story is more easily applicable to us today than to his contemporaries. Wherever you are on this journey, I hope that you will interact profoundly with God, taking the *Jacob journey* in its essence and letting God access the deep recesses of your heart.

The message for Illini basketball players during their

2005 NCAA championship bid communicates a message for us as we begin a study of the epic story of Jacob.
*Only as far as I look, can I see.* . . . I want you to see further.
*Only as much as I dream, can I be* . . . . I want you to dream more clearly.
*Inside everyone is a champion.* . . . *Seek, and ye shall find him.* I want you to become that champion to the glory of God!
Rabbi Zusya's quote is like a headlight that shines all the way to the end of our study.

"In the coming world, they will not ask me: 'Why were you not Moses?'
They will ask me: 'Why were you not Zusya?'"

Walk with Jacob and you will find a model that will point you to becoming who and what you can be in such a way that it will be enough in your life now and beyond in the coming world. This is what God created you for. Let Jacob point the way.

**Response**

Prayer that you may receive what is meant for you.

# PART ONE

# JOURNEYING

# CHAPTER 1

# WOMB WITH A VIEW – PURPOSE PACKAGED IN A PERSON

*For You created my inmost being; You knit me together in my mother's womb. Your eyes saw my unformed body. All the days ordained for me were written in Your book before one of them came to be.*

*Psalm 139:13, 16*

*And Isaac was forty years old when he took Rebekah, the daughter of Bethuel the Aramean from Paddan-aram, and sister of Laban the Aramean, to be his wife. Isaac prayed to the Lord on behalf of his wife, because she was barren; and the LORD answered him and Rebekah his wife conceived. But the children struggled together within her; and she said, "If it is so, why then am I this way?"*
*So she went to inquire of the LORD. The LORD said to her, "Two nations are in your womb;*
*And two peoples will be separated from your body;*
*And one people shall be stronger than the other;*
*And the older shall serve the younger."*

*Genesis 25:20-23*

*There is a feeling that I have a destiny far away from the shallow and preposterous posing that is our life.*

*Kurt Vonnegut, Jr.*

# WOMB WITH A VIEW –
# PURPOSE PACKAGED IN A PERSON

In *A Room with a View,* the 1908 novel by E. M. Forster, two men and a single woman with her aunt as chaperone determine who will get the hotel room that has a view of beautiful Florence, Italy. The men prevail on the women to exchange rooms. The ladies gain the benefit of the room with a commanding vista.

## What Do You See from Your Window?

What is your *room with a view?* What is the place, the platform, the perspective from which you look at life? You have one. What is it? *If you fail to grasp the bigger plan or purpose for your life, the view from your room will never fill you up but rather will always let you down.*

Almost 4,000 years ago one of the most important men in all of history demonstrated a lesson that can mean the difference between failure or success for today's leader. Jacob lived this lesson in a dramatic way, and his life journey has become the epic story of how God works to develop a leader *from birth to death.* No other character in the Bible provides this life-long perspective.

The principles in Jacob's story are so powerful that any leader can be impacted and permanently changed by them. Jacob's life can help mold and challenge your conclusions about the perspective you have adopted for your life.

My friend Cole found this to be true. As we sat together in the coffee shop one day, I noted that Cole appeared flat, confused, and somewhat discouraged. From an external perspective this seemed surprising. He is lean and athletic. He has a beautiful wife who is a recognized leader in their church. His two young sons are the delight of his life. He also enjoys the heritage of an outstanding Christian home.

Working for a financial firm in Chicago, Cole took an assignment in Asia. Because he caught a financial wave, he was soon making seven figures a year and retired at twenty-nine to do what he wanted for the rest of his life.

Why wasn't he fulfilled and deeply satisfied? He was living the dream of entrepreneurs and business leaders, the *room with a view* that others wish for. What was wrong?

It was simple. His *room with a view* did not provide what he needed deep in his soul. Even though he was financially set for life, he lacked a sense of purpose and meaning. Cole had not yet acquired the lessons that the life of Jacob teaches. No room with a view (not even the largest and best corner office) can fill the soul if a person is disconnected from the larger purposes of life.

Geoff Bellman is clearly in touch with the reality reflected in Jacob's life. From his perspective as a successful consultant, he writes:

> The prevailing "wisdom" of corporate life says that if you cannot measure it, it is not important. I disagree. I believe that if it's important, you cannot measure it. The really important things in life cannot be measured, made tangible, quantified, packaged, boxed, or tied down. In fact, the most important things in life are not "things" at all. What we want out of life is not for sale, for lease, or for rent (p. 106).

Jacob's life demonstrates the necessity of a life plan and purpose. What is surprising is how early it shows up in his life–it is *prenatal!*

### It's Never Too Early!

The Bible book of Genesis is organized around *generations,* the succeeding waves of people who inhabit the earth. In Genesis 25 Jacob is introduced in the context of the generations of his grandfather, Abraham, and his father, Isaac. Much is made of his heritage as, time after time in Scripture, God identifies Himself as the God of *Abraham, Isaac and Jacob*. Through Isaac, Jacob is connected to the promises given to Abraham. He is irrevocably linked to those who came before him as well as to those who will follow him. As such, Jacob is representative of all leaders. Leaders must see their lives in the context of those who come before them with a vision for those who will come after them. They need to be sensitive to their legacy while investing their lives and efforts in their current and following generations.

Though Jacob was the link between the promises given to his grandfather, father and the generations to follow, he faced one crisis after another. The first crisis associated with Jacob was prenatal! His mother, Rebekah, was failing to conceive a child (Genesis 25:19-21). Without a son, the prophecies given to Abraham and Isaac of a large nation coming from them would prove empty. It's no wonder Isaac prayed earnestly for a child (Genesis 25:21), interceding powerfully on behalf of Rebekah with the result that she finally conceived.

This ecstatic period of Rebekah's life was not followed by an easy pregnancy. Nothing was ever trouble-free where Jacob was concerned. It became apparent that Rebekah was carrying twins. A fearful situation developed when the sensations inside her indicated they were fighting each other. She followed Isaac's example and went directly to God in prayer, pleading to know what was happening. The answer to her prayer was dramatic! "Two nations are in your womb; and two peoples shall be separated from your body; and one people shall be stronger than the other; and the older shall serve the younger" (Genesis 25:22-23).

The response to Rebekah's anxiety over the struggle within her was a pronouncement which outlines the history and contribution of her two sons before they were even born. Each was destined to be the progenitor of a separate nation, but Jacob was to be the stronger one. Contrary to ancient custom, the older twin would be subservient to the younger. Jacob was postmarked before birth to lead a chosen people.

I believe the purpose of the two children was specified for Rebekah's benefit. Now, if she were asked at a well-side meeting of her friends if she believed there was any real purpose for a second child when the first always took first place, she had an answer. "The younger will be the father of a great nation." She could add, "I know this baby is part of the plan that the Lord gave to his grandfather, Abraham and my husband, Isaac." Beatrix Potter says quaintly that "babies are such a beautiful way to start people." This baby is beginning his journey as a human being labeled with purpose!

In this study of a great Old Testament character, we are following Jacob's life formation from birth to death to see what it teaches us. The first thing we discover is that his life was lived under a clear and powerful *purpose*. For readers 4,000 years removed from Jacob's life, the principle is the same. A deep awareness of *our* purpose will encourage us to fulfill our destiny. Without grasping the idea there is a bigger plan for our lives, we will be unfulfilled, no matter how much money or power we accumulate.

## Birth Pains

A compelling sense of purpose may require a deeply trying period of life to know it. St. John of the Cross referred to such times as the "dark night of the soul." I gained a more passionate and focused sense of mission during a bleak part of my life. Here is part of my story.

While serving as academic dean for a small Christian college in Virginia, I was pushed out when the school changed its direction and focus. My family was uprooted with two major moves as I scrambled for work. Short-term jobs such as a chaplain in a college and then in a correctional institution, an adjunct faculty member for a Christian college and other short-term miscellaneous activities were all I could find. This long unsettled transition period seemed to be leading nowhere. Every career door closed in my face. To memorialize this time, I kept a thick file of inquiries and rejections. I was a forgotten man in my career, and my grief and confusion felt overwhelming. Yet, I believe this period was an essential anteroom which moved me, amidst my pain, to a life which now makes the losses of that time seem inconsequential.

Slowly I began to know more deeply why I had been born. The diverse array of personal experiences–including formal biblical and theological training, hundreds of hours of counseling and caring for others at deep levels of their lives, the pain of rejection and the powerful realities of my own journey–had prepared me for a unique contribution. I was to take this unusual life package and translate it into leveraged opportunities for others.

This purpose was confirmed to me by a verse in the Psalms, "And even when I am old and gray, O God, do not forsake me, until I declare Your strength to this generation, Your power to all who are to come" (Psalm 71:18). At last I could verbalize it! "Whatever else may happen, however narrow or wide my circle of influence, my life contribution must involve taking what has been entrusted to me and sharing it with as many as I possibly can."

Working on the big picture for my life reminds me of taking a trip and looking at the map to make sure you are remembering the route. It takes away that uncomfortable feeling about making a wrong turn when you have only a few seconds to make a decision with six lanes of traffic in front of you. I wrote down conclusions about my *purpose (why* I am living), *vision (what* I hope to accomplish), and *mission (how* I hope to realize this). This project has been valuable for me and has a settling effect every time I think about it or update it for a new year. It helps eliminate uncertainty and encourages the clarity I need to keep from wandering.

**People of Purpose–Jacob and You**
Four thousand years ago, before Jacob was ever born, his life was branded with *purpose.* There was never a possibility that Jacob would live one day of his life without an established purpose overshadowing him. This is supposed to be our experience as well. A deep sense of purpose and plan is like an implanted gyroscope to help keep us steady and keel-down in the fierce waves and storms which confront us.

Philosophers speak passionately about purpose as foundational for living. Thomas Carlyle wrote:

A man with a half-volition . . . makes no way on the smoothest road; a man with a whole volition advances on the roughest, and will reach his purpose, if there be even a little wisdom in it; the man without a purpose is like a ship without a rudder–a no man. Have a purpose in life, and, having it, throw such strength of mind and muscle into your work as God has given you (p. 534).

This is perhaps the genius of Jacob's life. He pursued the program, plan, and purpose for his life, no matter what came his way. From the time he grabbed his brother's heel at birth until he tucked his feet up on the bed and died, Jacob lived with purpose!

The hunger today to know the *why* of our lives makes it no accident that a book like *The Purpose Driven Life–What on Earth Am I Here For?* by Rick Warren became a phenomenal bestseller. Like our look at Jacob, it is more than a self-help book or a positive mental attitude boost. If you are confused about the Plan, Purpose, the Big Picture for your life, use a book like this. Talk to your Designer about why He placed you on planet earth. Any one of numerous purpose statements in the Bible can become a powerful force in your life. The basics of life purpose are there. Find another person to walk with you in your quest for greater clarity about your life.

As we share the journey with Jacob, we can sharpen our focus so that we will permanently live our lives on a higher plane! Like Jacob, we are called to *a life with a view*. When our life is viewed from the perspective of God's purpose for us, something deep and powerful will take place within the everyday details of our existence.

Some years ago an ad campaign for Southwest Airlines exclaimed, "You are now free to move about the country." With a clear sense of our purpose, we are free to move about the opportunities that come our way, knowing that we are making a unique contribution and living a distinctive life!

## THE LEADER'S JOURNEY ...
### It begins with purpose!

Questions for Reflection (alone or in a group):

1.  Have you come to a sense of purpose for your life? Have you written it out?

2.  What circumstances were most influential in developing your sense of destiny, plan or purpose? How did you come to this understanding?

3.  How can a person discover a sharper purpose for living?

4.  Do you need to discuss with another person the purpose and plan for your life and how well you are fulfilling it?

5.  What is one action step that will help drill the reality of a "purpose driven life" more deeply into your consciousness?

6.  Jacob began his life with a special heritage. Do you have a legacy that has helped direct you to the plan or purpose for your life?

**Response**

Praise and worship that God has given you your being and a purpose.

# CHAPTER 2

# YOUR PERSONAL PACKAGE – HOW YOU ARE WIRED

*The world has many kings, but only one Michelangelo.*
*Arentino, a contemporary of Michelangelo*

*When her days to be delivered were fulfilled, behold, there were twins in her womb. Now the first came forth red, all over like a hairy garment; and they named him Esau. Afterward his brother came forth with his hand holding onto Esau's heel, so his name was called Jacob.*
*Genesis 25:24-26*

*A person is a person insofar as he has a secret . . .*
*of his own that cannot be communicated to anyone else . . .*
*the secrecy, the hiddenness,*
*the solitude of his own individual being,*
*which God alone can penetrate and understand.*
*Thomas Merton*

# YOUR PERSONAL PACKAGE – HOW YOU ARE WIRED

Sometimes the details in biblical stories are surprising and confusing. This chapter is built around one of them–Jacob grabbing his twin brother's heel as they were born. Is it just a vivid detail in an ancient Hebrew story or is there something significant here? Could it be that this obscure incident in Jacob's life is making a powerful statement to people today?

Not many leaders take time to review their lives to see what makes them run with the wolves like they do. More should. This book is aimed at the depths of your life versus what you do to push an organization (business, nonprofit, church) to its limits. Jacob provides the core for our considerations while we surround his story with our own experiences. The stories of select business leaders are interwoven (names changed) throughout the book.

## The Lucky Sperm Club

Jay may be the only company president of a family-owned business in the United States who is a fourth generation president and a Ph.D. He is a member of the "Lucky Sperm Club," that special group who lead family-owned companies. I was curious about the conversations that typically take place when they meet, so I asked what they talk about. Do they talk about their *purpose*? Do they consider the reasons they are privileged to carry on a family legacy as presidents of these family-owned businesses? Do they share perspectives on how well they are suited to be presidents or CEOs? Are they leading the family company because it fell in their laps or because they can do it better than any other available persons? In other words, do they see themselves as uniquely qualified to be in the leadership positions they are in?

I was disappointed to learn that the usual topics of discussion for this elite group centered on the nuts and bolts of family businesses. These big-picture issues never came up.

## Wired or Not

This was not the case with Alex (whom we meet again in chapter 4). In a meeting with other business owners, he shared a current challenge. Salary negotiations with a pushy new employee were a real problem. One of the group asked why he had not delegated this volatile matter to a vice president. He responded immediately, "No one else in the company is wired to be a CEO."

That's it! Alex knows he is "wired to be a CEO." He is one of a handful of presidents I know who have taken their family company, run it better and developed it far beyond their fathers' capacity to do so.

James is another CEO who is superbly suited to lead his die-casting firm. He took his father's company into a new era despite the fact that other materials competed with aluminum, and business was being shipped overseas to Japan, China and the Pacific Rim. He made the sharp changes in business necessary for survival. His reputation is such that he became president of his national trade association and directed a staff of people in Chicago from his company in downstate Illinois.

Both men were not only trained from the bottom up. They are wired for what they do. They have a fit that everybody knows is right.

## Your Software Package Was Running Before
## You Knew It

How are *you* wired? What kind of software package is inscribed on the hard drive of your humanity?

Think about the moment before your first breath was drawn, while you were hanging upside down being slapped on the rear for your first cry. What was your wiring? Recall early memories as a child. What do you sense they are telling you? You may not want to revisit your childhood, but you may need to do so. There is strong biblical precedent for careful reflection on our earliest memories. David imagined his prenatal state in Psalm 139 to marvel and worship. When Jesus hung on the cross, He thought of the great Messianic Psalm 22, which references the early days of life in verses 9-10.

Yet You are He who brought me forth from the womb;
You made me trust when upon my mother's breasts.
Upon You I was cast from birth;
You have been my God from my mother's womb.

When God informed Jeremiah, a nondescript priest from an insignificant isolated village northeast of Jerusalem, about his call to be a powerful, public and influential prophet, He knew that Jeremiah would have trouble buying into the idea. His word to Jeremiah was, "Before I formed you in the womb I knew you, and before you were born I consecrated you" (Jeremiah 1:5). An amplified paraphrase might read, "I installed your software package. I took care of your internal architecture. I determined what I was going to do with your life before you were born! Though you think I have come to the wrong person in your little village, I wired you before you knew what was there."

Contemplating our past is an appropriate exercise for those who wish to explore more fully the dimensions of their human existence. Perhaps some of us have things in our package we have missed. It would be a shame if we did not become aware of our wiring and live it out. Being fully in touch with our internal architecture and living accordingly may mean a journey back in time, a journey to our earliest memories.

**A Personal Journey Back in Time**

My journey back to childhood memories was prodded along by Carole. We were meeting in the beautiful basilica on the campus of Notre Dame University to discuss Jacob's story. I was trying to explain to Carole why I found the life of Jacob so compelling. She is a successful writer and consultant and said something that jarred me, "Charles, you haven't gone deep enough. Though you have spent years studying the life of Jacob, there is something you haven't connected with yet. Why don't you walk around the church alone and think."

Somewhat dazed and confused, I did so. One memory that surfaced was a casual exchange I had had with a young woman in a Quebec bookstore. She made a passing remark, "It is a shame to see a man thirty-five who still hasn't figured out who he is." Her comment was painful even though it was not directed at me. Slowly it began to dawn on me that I was not connecting with Jacob's life at a deep level because I was not connecting with my *own*. I was not secure and confident of my identity. I was out of touch with my wiring. What Parker Palmer wrote was true of me, "We arrive in this world with birthright gifts–then we spend the first half of our lives abandoning them or letting others disabuse us of them" (p.12).

The net result was a return to my boyhood, where I got behind the curtain, which was filtering out light from this preschool period of my life. What I found resembled old snapshots you find in a drawer. The first snapshot moment was from the morning my father took me with him on a horse-drawn hayrake and balanced me on the seat with him. When my ankle got caught in the lever, which raised and lowered the curved steel prongs that turned over the hay, my dad took me off the rake, put his leather gloves beneath my ankle, and gently supported my injured ankle. Why is this memory so vivid, like an impressionist painting with the warmth and golden splendor of the sunlit field? Why do I remember the details of leather gloves and my father's loving touch? It's simple. I am wired for caring relationships. Put this wiring of nurturing relationships with the spiritual gift of encouragement, and many years of professional and personal practice, and I am who I am today.

The next snapshot is a picture of a small boy standing by a hay pile, pitchfork in hand. This single picture is now fleshed out in the life of a project/process person who thrives on a variety of meaningful or strategic projects which contribute to a bigger goal. I love to throw my energy into "stacking-hay kinds of projects" such as partnering with a client in significant ways, producing materials or developing a program born out of a creative vision. After stepping back to appreciate it for a little while, I am ready to move on to the next project. The little boy standing by the hay he stacked is still making haystacks and stopping for a short time to admire them! They just look different now.

On another occasion, when my father spoke of dreading to go out at night to get a hired hand, I appeared in a few moments with his coat on backwards dragging the ground and said, "Daddy, I'll go for you." Freeze the frame! It's who I am today after spiritual gifting is added to the package. I want to serve, meet the needs of others and build deeply into their lives. Why? It's my software package!

Parker Palmer, a nationally known educator, leader, and writer, took a long and circuitous journey and came to this conclusion: "Teaching, I was coming to understand, is my native way of being in the world. Make me a cleric or CEO, a poet or politico, and teaching is what I will do. Teaching is at the heart of my vocation and will manifest itself in any role I play" (p. 21). Have you come to similar clarity? Have you clicked on the icon yet with your name on it to see what appears on your memory screen? Perhaps a look at Jacob in his prenatal venue will prod you to do so.

**One "Heel" of a Story**

Our journey with Jacob has a single focus–looking at the life formation of a leader from birth to death in order to gain insight for our own lives. This means we can't skip the crucial umbilical cord stage of his story. The insight we gain here encourages us to connect with who we were from birth. The details of the birth of Esau and Jacob are recorded in Genesis 25:24-26.

When her days to be delivered were fulfilled, behold, there were twins in her womb. Now the first came forth red, all over like a hairy garment; and they named him Esau. Afterward his brother came forth with his hand holding on to Esau's heel, so his name was called Jacob; and Isaac was sixty years old when she gave birth to them.

Near East scholars agree that the birth events often determined the names of children. Esau was born with an unusual amount of hair. *Hypertrichosis* might have been written on his medical chart today. His ruddy or reddish appearance earned him the name, Esau. As an infant, Esau looked the part of who he eventually became–a rugged outdoorsman and patriarch of the "red nation" named after him, Edom, or modern day Jordan.

As a rule, babies are passively involved in the birth process. Surviving the trauma of delivery is their one task. Things were different, however, with Jacob. Before he saw the light of day, he was grabbing the heel of his brother! This unusual incident is like looking through the sights of a rifle to see the projectile of his entire life. He is the heel grabber who claws his way all the way through life until he magnificently fulfills his destiny. It is as if the prenatal prophecy, which established his purpose, was programmed into the birth process. His response seems to have been,

"Okay, let's get on with it. Esau may be firstborn, but he won't get ahead of me. I've got him by the heel." As a result, he was given the name Jacob. *Jacob* is a shortened form of the Hebrew phrase, "May God protect," but sounds like the Hebrew word *heel*. His name takes on the idea of "the grabber."

Later in life Esau felt the full effects of his heel-grabbing brother. After Jacob stole both his birthright and his blessing, Esau angrily exclaimed, "Is he not rightly called named Jacob, for he has supplanted me these two times? He took away my birthright, and behold, now he has taken away my blessing" (Genesis 27:36).

Hundreds of years later the prophet Hosea began Jacob's story with the heel-grabbing incident, "In the womb he took his brother by the heel, and in his maturity he contended with God" (12:3).

Jacob's recorded history in Genesis, in which he begins to act out his destiny before he is born, reminds me of John the Baptist, forerunner of Jesus Christ. When Mary was carrying baby Jesus, she visited her cousin Elizabeth who was six months pregnant with John. When Mary greeted her, baby John leaped for joy within Elizabeth's womb. John's purpose was to announce the arrival of the Jewish Messiah. Before either was born, John was doing his best to proclaim the uniqueness of Jesus!

From the moment he grabbed his brother's heel in the birth process until he finally became the man he could be–Israel, prince with God, Jacob had internal software that made him drastically different from his brother, Esau. Each of us has something uniquely inscribed in our humanity that is never duplicated precisely in another human being. Jacob's software package was running at birth. What is operating in you?

## Through the Eyes of a Goose

A Canadian goose helped me understand the absurdity of looking at ourselves superficially without considering what is wired deeply in our being. Each spring, entering the doors in the center of a sweeping semi-circular glass expanse became an adventure for employees of a company where I occupied office space. A pair of Canadian geese had set up housekeeping near the entrance in a raised ivy-covered area, which included a birch tree. The female removed the ivy, made a nest and laid her eggs. Her mate stood guard, hissed at everyone who came by, and occasionally dive-bombed someone with his five-foot wing span. During the day, hour after hour, he stood in front of the glass and pecked at it, leaving smudge marks from his beak. One day I knelt down and looked into the window just like he did to understand his actions. He was pecking at his image reflected in the glass!

He reminded me of the Bible verse which says, "For now we see in a mirror dimly, but then face to face; now I know in part, but then I shall know fully just as I also have been fully known" (1 Corinthians 13:12). Because that gander wasn't getting a clear picture of reality, he never changed his pecking habit.

What about the leader who only sees his image as reflected in the windows of the corner office, or from the TV clip highlighting his career, or on the cover of a magazine? Is he like the goose who can't see beyond what is mirrored as reality and never gets beyond a mere surface reflection?

Greg Maddux, pitcher for the Chicago Cubs, tells it like it is as an athlete. Before he won his 300th game on August 7, 2004 (some baseball experts think he will be the last pitcher to do so), he said in an interview, "When I look at myself in the mirror, I will be the same person whether I win 299 games or 305."

**Finally**

Neither your life nor mine can be fully formed until we know, accept and live into our God-given personal wiring. What King David said 3000 years ago speaks powerfully to present day leaders who are pressured to merge identity with role.

For You formed my inward parts;
You wove me in my mother's womb.
Your eyes have seen my unformed substance;
And in Your book were all written
The days that were ordained for me,
When as yet there was not one of them.
(Psalm 139:13, 16)

David went back to his infancy to see his personhood and being as a gift from God.

Paul the Apostle did not speak of himself as a self-made leader, but of the One "who had set me apart even from my mother's womb, and called me through His grace" (Galatians 1:15).

Jacob seemed to know instinctively how he was wired. Do you? If you take a journey back in time, you may discover something rich and meaningful. For example:

1. When you let yourself be stripped for the moment of everything that surrounds or suffocates your life, you may recognize that not only your presence on the earth but also your personhood comes from God. It is humbling.

2. You gain freedom to live as the singularly great person God made you to be. "I am not an independent, self-made person; I am a dependent person privileged with opportunities to learn, develop and grow into the person God made me to be when I entered the world."

3. You will not get trapped in the confused identity of mixing up who you are with what you now do. You *are*, I

*am*–whatever we *might do*. The Psalmist said, "I am fear-fully and wonderfully made" (Psalm 139:14). He didn't say, "I made myself fearfully and wonderfully."

4. Leaving this earth will be easier since you have already looked at yourself as the total person God made you to be without anything else you have accumulated along the way. When the externals of our lives are stripped away, we won't be denuded.

5. Because Jacob lived out his personal architecture (wiring), he was able to fully live *into* the various periods of his life. He was intensely engaged in living each stage of his life. While he seemed to do very well just hanging around in his early years, he was relentlessly opportunistic with Esau. He was an unabashed romantic with Rachel and managed a large household with the four women with whom he fathered the children who became the nation of Israel. Resourcefulness was built into him and he deployed it superbly in partnership with God in Laban's household. He rose to new heights in his final years because he knew what his life was all about.

THE LEADER'S JOURNEY . . .
**Cooperating with the gift of his or her personal architecture (wiring) instead of trying to be like someone else or fit into the wrong kind of mold**

Questions for Reflection (alone or in a group)

1. How do you react to this chapter?

2. Are you able to go back to a much earlier time in your life and understand more of your personal package which is essentially who you are now in your more mature and developed state?

3. Describe some elements of your personal package.

4. Do you know enough about who you are and how you are wired so that you are cooperating with your personal package instead of conflicting with it?

5. Is there something you need to follow up or act on in light of your personal wiring?

**Response**

Praise for your uniqueness and prayer that you will be able to live out your potential.

# CHAPTER 3

# FAMILY FORMATION –
# WHAT BENT YOUR BRANCHES?

+≈≈+

*Home is the seminary of all other institutions.*
*E. H. Chapin*


*So the boys grew, and Esau was a skillful hunter,*
*a man of the field;*
*but Jacob was a mild man, dwelling in tents.*
*And Isaac loved Esau because he ate of his game,*
*but Rebekah loved Jacob.*
*Genesis 25:27-28*


*What shapes me?*
*What makes me?*

*Should I even ask the question?*

*What are the events, the influences,*
*the experiences that shaped my life?*

*Who have been the sculptors?*

*Did my dad ask these questions
or are they only the trend of this generation?*
                                    Andrew Costello

# FAMILY FORMATION –
# WHAT BENT YOUR BRANCHES?

I live near Chicago–the "Windy City." Though the description originally applied to its politicians, we do get our share of windy days. A bike trail that passes near my house is lined with trees for the majority of its forty-mile loop. When I ride on the trail I observe two phenomena in the trees. Some have been bent by the winds that blow almost incessantly from the west. Others bend toward the bike path to get more sunlight. In both cases there is clear evidence that the trees have felt the effect of their environment.

## Bending Branches

We are using the lens of Jacob's life to capture key aspects of the formation in the life of a leader. Through this lens we have seen that we have a purpose, given to us by God even before we were born. We also have a wiring that enables us to live out our purpose, and like the trees on the bike trail, we too are influenced by our environment. This influence of family is the subject of this chapter.

*Becoming who you can be* and *doing what you can do* takes a lifetime. That lifetime began even before your birth. Who you are and where you are today is impacted by what you experienced while growing up. Some of us carry wounds, distortions or hindrances from the past that hold us back today. I was reminded of this by a mission executive who said that recruiting missionaries today is a more difficult process because of problems from earlier experiences that still plague candidates. Many of us, in contrast, can directly attribute our level of success to the powerful influence of our family of origin.

*Maximizing our family heritage requires that we recognize and gain energy from both the positives **and** negatives.* But this is not easy, as Preston so graphically demonstrated.

## Succeeding Wounded

When I contacted Preston about the LifeServe Mentoring program, I guessed it was unlikely he would consider himself a candidate. He was extraordinarily successful in business. I learned later that he was the youngest man in the world to build a business of his size in his industry. He employed several six-figure income Ph.Ds and senior executives. He hired the best consultants. He was a member of two CEO groups–one secular and the other dedicated to helping Christian CEOs integrate biblical principles and business acumen.

He had a shelf of excellent give-away books for other leaders. He and his wife conducted a Bible study in their home. From his company newsletter it was clear that he was a master team-builder who had integrated both faith and business principles, creating structures in which employees found fulfillment and productivity.

Preston was willing to consider my offer, and so I inventoried his concerns and was surprised at what he put high on his list–*woundedness!* Of course, there were other pressure points in his life, such as the need for a high level hire who would lead the charge to maintain the company growth rate of 20 percent, which had been registered every year for the past decade. But why woundedness?

His story emerged painfully and slowly. He was the oldest of six children. His father was dashing and handsome and always involved in a business venture. His mother anchored the family with love and care, embracing each of the children in their Roman Catholic home. But there was a very dark side to the family as well. His father was an alcoholic whose drinking escapades kept the children in a state of fear and uncertainty. One evening a police chase ended at their home with his drunken father avoiding jail only because of his ability to talk his way out of jams.

The one opportunity for bonding between Preston and

his dad was baseball. After an injury ended Preston's ability to play ball, his father always looked at him as damaged property.

The family was shattered when his mother died and his only reliable source of love and support was gone. Things became intolerable in their troubled home when the welfare of the children was left to his father. Lacking any other alternatives, Preston took an unprecedented move. He sued for custody of his siblings. Because of his nurturing and caring spirit, Preston's investment in his younger siblings paid off remarkably well. Most are committed Christians. His one sister, who seemed destined for a troubled life, is now a respected missionary with her husband.

Taking care of his brothers and sisters taught Preston many valuable lessons, which he transferred to his company. He became a phenomenal team-builder who sacrificed himself for others. He was a powerful motivator who could rally his employees to great accomplishments and profits.

But all of this came at a high personal price. Preston was acting out of his woundedness as much or more than he was acting out of his health. *Receiving* care, concern, nurture and love was difficult. He feared intimacy even in the face of a strong and committed marriage. His financial and business success had not succeeded in healing his wounds from early childhood. He was a man with a purpose and obvious abilities, but his "branches had been bent" by the prevailing winds of his family of origin.

## Growing and Becoming

None of us is impervious to the totality of what happened while we were being formed in our home environments. Preston wasn't. I wasn't. Jacob wasn't. Even though some have enjoyed a more healthy home life than others, none of us grew up in perfect environments. There is good and the not-so-good in *every* family.

What are we to do with the positives and the negatives of our past? The life of Jacob helps us interpret these background elements of our lives. Jacob's most formative years are compressed into two verses: "So the boys grew, and Esau became a skillful hunter, a man of the field; but Jacob was a mild man, dwelling in tents. And Isaac loved Esau because he ate of his game, but Rebekah loved Jacob" (Genesis 25:27-28).

These verses capture a universal paradigm that works its way out in every family. The first part of the paradigm is what took place in the boys–they *grew* and, as a result, *became*. They traveled very different roads and wound up in very different places. The second part of the paradigm is found in the responses of the parents toward the twins. Isaac loved Esau, but Rebekah loved Jacob.

The first component of this paradigm is found in the simple but profound statement, "So the boys grew." Thousands of changes take place as a child grows. Even though you may not remember a single event from birth to the time you began to walk and talk, you were being formed. Your branches were being bent.

The second component of this home model from Jacob and Esau indicates another critical aspect of how our lives took shape. It says, "Esau *became* . . . and Jacob *was*." Something happened to each. They emerged. They developed. They became. Their personalities and individualities emerged. We are persons who can be described by our unique attributes and characteristics.

Esau is characterized by his activities. Life attributes or character are the brush strokes used for Jacob. Differences depict this family, differences in the brothers, differences in their development, and differences in family loyalties and life directions. Genesis 25:27 is one of the most complete one-sentence portraits of two individuals in the Bible: "When the boys grew up, Esau became a skillful hunter, a man of the field; but Jacob was a peaceful man, living in tents."

I can't read the few words about Esau without feeling his vigor, energy and ruggedness. Pictures of his roaming remote areas leap out of the text. Folklore contains epic stories of men such as Esau–men of the outdoors, adventure, exploration, and the hunt.

Jacob is harder to visualize from the short description given. But in the culture of that day, a "tent dweller" was a man of culture, more "civilized" than the man of the open field. The Hebrew word translated "peaceful" supports this conclusion in that in other contexts the word has the idea of "complete, sound, wholesome, even-tempered" (Genesis 20:5, 6; Job 1:8; 2:3). In the significant contrast in how the two brothers developed, each began to live out his purpose. Each was wired for his unique destiny.

**"She Loves Me. . . He Loves Me Not"**

Only one feature is selected concerning the home environment in which the differences of the twins became pronounced. However, this feature is pivotal in their development. Jacob loved Esau. Rebekah loved Jacob. The home in which Esau and Jacob grew and developed is one characterized by open favoritism. But that is not the only negative in this home. We read that Esau was loved by his father because, as one commentator vividly says, Esau "put venison in his father's mouth."

Was this reason enough to love Esau? Appreciate him, yes, but love or favor him because he could hunt? No! Acceptance should not be given because of a child's ability to feed either the body or ego of a parent. When acceptance is based on catering to the whims or emotional needs of parents, a child will always hunger for a deeper and truer relationship. Esau's later choices indicate a continuing need for acceptance. When Jacob left home, Esau attempted to emulate Jacob and could gain his parents' approval with a second and more satisfactory marriage (his first marriage troubled both parents, and Rebekah spoke vehemently against it: Genesis 26:34-35; 27:46; 28:7-9).

The conditional acceptance felt by Esau is the experience of many men today. Books address this issue, and men's movements, both secular and religious, encourage men to explore the deep hole in their souls as a result of conditional love. I have a memory montage from the business leaders who share their stories with me.

I played alone a lot. I made things. I waited for my dad to come home and give me attention and see what I had done. It never happened. My older brother helped fill this father role that was missing from my dad.

My mother was a good woman. I was close to her and she loved me. She died. My father married a young woman who had no love for us. We had no relation with her whatsoever. My dad never gave me a word of encouragement. Once when we were on a working trip, I got so fed up and hurt so bad that I ran away. We had the one interchange of my life where I opened my heart to him to share how bad I felt about the way he was always running me down. He responded by saying, "That's the way it is. That's the way it was with my father too." With sadness, Jim noted how he still talks with his sister of the pain and emptiness of this relationship they had with their father.

I'm still trying to please my father by becoming a successful businessman. I need to have his "Well done, son" and get a real pat on the back from him. I want to hear him say that he is proud of me. But he is dead!

When I review their stories, I feel the pain with them. Like Esau, many men today feel unsure about themselves. Psychologists use such terminology as "weak ego structure" to describe this phenomenon. Esau apparently did not know "who he was" and unfortunately many more men have struggled with similar feelings. Ken Burns interviewed Mark McGwire after his 70-homerun season. Mark spoke of learning to open up his emotions and admitted to seeing a psychologist during a time of divorce and injury. "It took me twenty-eight years to try to start to figure out who I was. Can you imagine somebody that's, like, fifty years old that never started?"

But Esau was not the only son who did not connect with his father at a deep level. Virtually nothing is mentioned of Isaac's relationship with Jacob. This is surprising because Isaac and Jacob were similar in their personalities. Both were inward, contemplative, home-centered and God-conscious. Esau had none of these inclinations. Maybe Isaac's attraction to Esau was the toughness and courage which he seemed to lack. In any event, neither Esau *nor* Jacob received the kind of love they needed from their father.

In contrast to Esau's experience we read that Rebekah loved Jacob. Period! Why did she love Jacob? Of course, she felt close to him because he was the son, according to prenatal prophecy, whose future was to stand at the headwaters of a chosen nation. But the text suggests that she loved him "just because she did" (the contrast in the nature of the love is highlighted with the word *but*).

Esau experienced a conditional love from his father. The love Jacob experienced from his mother was unconditional. Jacob got the best end of the bargain. He got his mother. In his book on Jacob, *The Man Who Wrestled with*

*God: Light from the Old Testament on the Psychology of Individuation*, John Sanford makes an incisive comment: "Rebekah's love for Jacob gave to his personality a fundamental reservoir of psychological strength which later on stood him in good stead. A person who has been loved as a child has a core of emotional reserve and strength which is irreplaceable" (p. 81).

This unconditional love made it natural for Rebekah to share her own burning knowledge of God's plan for Jacob. His supreme function in life was to be the progenitor or forefather of the nation through which God would work out His purposes in the world. His family, which became the twelve tribes of Israel, was absolutely critical to God's plan for the rest of human history. Jacob caught the divine vision for his life.

## Negatives AND Positives

Every home has a mixture of good and not-so-good. All life formation has both pleasant and unpleasant experiences. We have highlighted some of the more challenging negatives of Jacob's home environment. There were, however, some very important positives, the most important one being the spiritual underpinning of the home. It was thoroughly monotheistic in the middle of a polytheistic, pagan Canaanite environment. God's call to Jacob's grandfather, Abraham, made a lasting difference. Though there were relational difficulties in the home, the reality of Yahweh, the one true God, was indisputable.

In addition to monotheism, the family lived in light of the covenant given to Abraham. They knew they were bound by God's promise to inherit the land and to be the channel of special divine blessing to the human race. This covenant reality was woven into the fabric of the home.

So, beneath the obvious negatives were deep and positive influences acting on the life of Jacob through both his father and mother. His home was flawed, but it was still functional. Jacob made the most of both kinds of influence. How did he do this?

**Wounds Plus Grace**

Because his story does not include the details of Jacob's process, it may be helpful for us to go back to Preston whose life formation included both positive and negatives. He suffered from a deep sense of woundedness despite his outstanding business success. Over time he became increasingly whole–a more complete person. We traced the process together. Here is part of what contributed to his healing.

I asked Preston to develop a chart with three columns. At the top of the columns were the following titles: *Areas of Woundedness; Results;* and *Wounds Plus Grace Equals Benefits.* I encouraged Preston to be thoroughly honest with himself. He had to open his memory to both the good and the not-so-good. He had to feel whatever needed to be felt.

With some encouragement Preston's first column (*Woundedness*) took shape-death of his mother, lack of connection with his father, his father's alcoholism, the stress of caring for his siblings. The list was long and painful.

The second column (*Results*) was not as bleak at it could have been, but it had many discouraging realities in it. Difficulty with intimacy, depression six months a year, weight gain, feelings of shame for being rejected because of his injury, seeking a father figure to fill a void . . . these were a few of the results of his woundedness.

The third column (*Wounds Plus Grace Equals Benefit*) took some thought, but soon began to overshadow the first two columns. For example, he took his father's entrepreneurial propensity to a much higher level, and without his father's fatal flaws, he went on to build a national reputation as a business leader.

To survive as a boy, he developed an unyielding

resistance and self-assurance. These characteristics became important positives when he was building a business in which he had to lead strong leaders, withstand attacks and setbacks, and compete against the giants of his industry.

The business arena can be unpredictable and crazily absurd at times. Preston's home life forced him to develop a tolerance for the surreal, abnormal and somewhat insane. When the police chased his father to their home, children in a normal family would have been terribly upset. In this family, the only question was whether the pizza was cheese or something else.

When so much was wrong, he became adept at visualizing and daydreaming as a means of creating something better than he was experiencing. This ability contributed to his success as a strategist. Even though he was featured on the cover of a national magazine, we didn't talk much about this. Rather, we talked about his current vision to reinvent or transform his company, to find a new paradigm so that its success didn't become its demise.

As we moved through the process of filling in the columns, we felt sadness but were also exhilarated by the sense of victory, opportunity, and destiny that came out of his background. Preston's childhood pit became a platform from which to move forward in adulthood. Though the prevailing winds of his home environment were not positive, Preston had ultimately grown tall and strong in spite of them. The same happened to Jacob.

Whatever happened in our formative years is good enough when it is given to God and integrated into our lives, instead of being hidden in the repressed darkness of the past. The wounds and broken areas of our lives are potential building blocks that provide an opportunity to ascend to greatness.

Our lives have been bent by the winds of our early years. Sometimes the emotional branches of our lives feel too bent to be tolerable to ourselves, much less helpful to others. But when we follow Jacob's story to its end, we will see how he bent to the light of God's grace despite everything in his past.

It's the phenomenon I observed with the trees on the forty-mile trail loop near our home. Yes, some of them were bent by the westerly winds. Others responded to a higher law. The bike trail offered access to the sunlight instead of shadows from other growth. They bent to the sun!

Jacob *received* the positives from his parents and the home they created. He *overcame* the negatives to find his destiny. He *persevered* in living out the realities and dimensions of his life for which he was prepared at home. Have you been able to do the same? How are your branches bent?

THE LEADER'S JOURNEY . . .
> **From our early years, integrating the positives and discovering potential from the negatives**

Questions for Reflection (alone or in a group):

1. As you look back, how do you feel about your growing up years?

2. What causes gratefulness or deep appreciation?

3. What causes pain or grief?

4. What did you gain from the positive things that prepared you for life?

5. Have you acquired benefits from the negative and limiting things? What limitations, if any, still persist?

6. In what way(s) might your life be affected by an insight from this chapter?

**Response**

Praise for what you gained in your family or home setting and trust in God to continue to bring good out of the negatives.

Evaluate your childhood home environment by filling in the chart:

ATTRIBUTE OR AREA                1(Least)          10(Most)

Contributions:
- Enriched
- Environment for growth
  and development
- Equipped
- Morals/character
- Self-image/personal
- Spiritual
- Emotional

Directed me:
- Positively
- Negatively

Determinative:
- Sufficient to prepare me
  for the life I am called
  to live

Your final comment?

# CHAPTER 4

# THE BIRTHRIGHT AND THE BLESSING – MAKING YOUR MOVE

*See to it that no man comes short of the grace of God . . . that there be no immoral or godless person like Esau, who sold his own birthright for a single meal.*

*Hebrews 12:15-16*

*But Jacob said, "First sell me your birthright." Then Jacob gave Esau bread and lentil stew; and he ate and drank, and rose and went on his way.*
*Thus Esau despised his birthright.*

*Genesis 25:31, 34*

*Now it came about, as soon as Isaac had finished blessing Jacob, and Jacob had hardly gone out from the presence of Isaac his father, that Esau his brother came in from his hunting . . . . Then he said, "Is he not rightly named Jacob, for he has supplanted me these two times? He took away my birthright, and behold, now he has taken away my blessing."*

*Genesis 27:30, 36*

*"The real test of a man is not when he plays the role that he wants for himself,*
*but when he plays the role destiny has for him."*
*Jan Patocka*

# THE BIRTHRIGHT AND THE BLESSING – MAKING YOUR MOVE

Put yourself in a meeting of business leaders at a retreat in the Rockies. You justified the expense to your company because the theme of the retreat matched a nagging concern of yours–*Getting Beyond Your Leadership to Your Life.*

In the first meeting, while the sun is setting behind the mountains, the leader speaks about choices which have brought you to the place where you are in your life. He explains, "During the next forty-eight hours we will do some careful thinking about our choices because they put us on the freeway of our lives. Some of us may need to pull into a 'rest area' and check a road map. Some may need to get off at the next exit. Others are facing tough times and need encouragement to stay the course."

The leader then breaks everyone into small groups with this assignment, "Identify the decisions which moved you onto the freeway of your life. What life choices help explain why you are here?" As your small group sits quietly to prepare their thoughts under the darkening sky, what response will you offer your weekend companions?

From the Genesis account, it seems plain what Jacob would answer if he were sitting in this reflective gathering of leaders. He made two choices which proved to be decisive, two entrance ramps that put him on his freeway of life. Before we consider Jacob's crucial life moves, I want to tell you about Alex. As a modern leader, his experience may help you identify the times when you *made your move.*

## Alex's Story

Alex is president and owner of a premier company in central Illinois. His financial sector corporation deals in large sums of money for a select and specialized client base.

He began his working life in typical fashion–emptying wastebaskets at six years of age in his father's business. When he went to college, his father made sure Alex had clients to service or sell. He was being groomed for the business early, consistently and progressively. In a few years Alex was running the company.

I was curious! "Alex, when did you realize that you were doing more than earning your allowance, that this was going to be your career?" His surprising response was that early in his life he saw his father's business as an opportunity to make a lot of money fast. His dream was an early retirement in Southern California.

But something happened to Alex that challenged his vision for life. His radical Christian conversion experience brought a very different perspective. "I realized the significance of career and profession and how important it is to God. I realized that I was designed or wired to do what I am doing for a purpose greater than an early retirement."

Alex grasped that life is about fulfilling a purpose, and that career and everything else must fit this. Coincidentally, through his mother, Alex can trace his lineage to Jacob. And, like Jacob, he realized his career was part of a much bigger plan.

When Jacob moved in to take Esau's inherited birthright and blessing, he probably saw an opportunity to get what he wanted without a full understanding of it.

There is no indication in the story that Jacob was particularly aware of his relationship with God on that day. It was just an *ordinary day*, but great turning points often occur unexpectedly. On this ordinary day Jacob may have been living temporarily at an outpost where shepherds were taking care of Isaac's flocks. Jacob may have cooked his own meals here. Some speculate that this meal was intended to serve as a trap for his brother, Esau, who had spent the entire day on an exhausting hunting trip.

When Esau returned to camp, he was famished and needed to eat and fast! "I've bonked," Esau might say if he were alive today. High-level bike riders use the term *bonk* when they run out of fuel on a ride (tour riders burn up to 10,000 calories per day). However, the text suggests that there was more happening to Esau than mere hunger. Something spiritual was also at work. When Jacob demanded Esau's birthright for a meal, Esau's response was cavalier. "What good is it if I starve in the process?" The deal was struck quickly. Esau got his meal and lost his birthright. Jacob leaped on his prize like a lion at the throat of a gazelle.

Wait a minute! Esau was probably bigger and stronger than Jacob. Maybe he could have just taken the food. Also, there had to be some other kind of food in the camp. But, no, it had to be Jacob's food, whatever the cost. Let tomorrow take care of itself. The comment about Esau eating his meal is instructive. Genesis 25:34 says, "He ate and drank." He enjoyed what he bargained for, "He got up." With a full stomach, it was over. "He went on his way." He got on with his life.

I tremble when I read this passage. I've made decisions just like Esau did. I've ignored long-term consequences in order to find short-term satisfaction. You no doubt have done the same. We have to admit sorrowfully that we could have been in Esau's place or worse and were only shielded providentially from our own folly.

Who could have guessed that on an ordinary day thousands of years ago, a meal would become a pivotal point, not only in the lives of two brothers, but in the lives of their descendents as well? Surely Esau didn't. I doubt if Jacob would have guessed it either.

The chapter ends with very sobering words: "Then Jacob gave Esau bread and lentil stew; and he ate and drank, and rose and went on his way. Thus Esau despised his birthright" (Genesis 25:34). This statement is strong, but the

New Testament restatement is more forceful yet:

> That there be no immoral or godless person like
> Esau, who sold his own birthright for a single meal.
> For you know that even afterwards, when he desired
> to inherit the blessing, he was rejected, for he found
> no place for repentance, though he sought for it with
> tears (Hebrews 12:16-17).

There is a final sad touch in the Genesis story. Esau
was destined to be the patriarch of a separate nation. He
ate the red lentil stew, and his name and his nation took on
this red name. Esau, the rugged, ruddy man, becomes Esau
the Red who will be father of the red nation, Edom. Esau
was on the freeway of his life with the impulsive food-for-
birthright decision.

But Jacob was also on the freeway of his life. He was
beginning to live out his destiny. Both men forged their
directions with their decisions. Their ordinary day was now
an extraordinary one.

**Risking All for a Blessing**

Some time later there was another decisive moment for
both Jacob and Esau in which their parents were involved.
Genesis 27 recounts the extraordinary event on another
ordinary day. Rebekah is the predator. Isaac is the hapless
head of the family. Jacob is the fearful participant and Esau
is once again the loser.

The precipitating event is Isaac's approaching death
before which he will give his formal *blessing* to the next
generation, his last will and testament. Custom dictated that
the oldest son be blessed with twice the amount of possessions and property than the younger son (the *birthright* in
Genesis 25 was about family priesthood and leadership).
Isaac commissioned Esau to go on a critically important

hunting trip to bring back wild game for a formal meal before the passing of the blessing.

Esau moved quickly and confidently. But perhaps this hunting trip reminded him of another one which had left him without his birthright. This time he was careful not to jeopardize the material blessing his father was ready to give to him.

However, while Esau was hunting, Rebekah made an extremely bold and risky maneuver for a woman in her culture–she intervened in the sacred rite of blessing. She was determined to change the beneficiary of the blessing from Esau to Jacob! Years before, as a young woman, she exhibited decisiveness and willingness to take on a risk when she made her choice to go with Abraham's servant to a foreign country to marry a man she had never met. After decades of marriage she was still willing to risk everything.

Why would Rebekah place herself in such a situation? Years before God had promised her that her younger son would become greater than her older son, that the older would serve the younger. Now, she was willing to do whatever she could to cooperate with God's purpose and plan for Jacob, however flawed her course of action. Her husband was choosing to ignore the divine promise. Perhaps it was because of his habit of indulging his appetite (the text points in this direction with the unusual phrase on Isaac's lips, "such as my soul desires" when he was telling Esau to fix his favorite meal). It was no secret why the son who was the hunter was his favorite! Rebekah, on the other hand, exercised great faith in the divine oracle when she put herself in harm's way for the sake of Jacob.

### Slick as Goat Hair

When Rebekah heard Isaac tell Esau to prepare to receive the firstborn inheritance, she went into crisis mode. Esau had already been disqualified from becoming the family leader when he sold his birthright, but he wanted the material possessions associated with such responsibility. Rebekah took matters in her own hands to make sure this did not happen.

Jacob told his mother that it would be reckless and dangerous for him to masquerade as Esau (Genesis 27:8-13), but Rebekah refused to take "no" for an answer. For years she had kept in mind the prenatal prophecy that God chose Jacob to be the preeminent one of the twins. Certain of what must be done, she assured Jacob that she would assume all liability if the plan failed.

She rapidly prepared a meal from the two goat kids Jacob snatched from the flocks and prepared Jacob to meet his father by putting Esau's best clothes on him along with goat hair for the back of his hands and his neck (we are told that the Romans used goat hair as a substitute for human hair). But there is one thing she couldn't prepare for–duplicating Esau's voice. How could a parent, particularly with children as different as Jacob and Esau, not distinguish the voice of one son from the other? However, if everything else in the scheme was plausible, blind Isaac might ignore the voice.

When Jacob took the meal to his father, the suspense was almost unbearable. What if Esau showed up? Isaac's suspicion was indicated by his question, "Why are you back so soon?" Jacob probably felt like a two-bit cheat when he replied, "Because the Lord your God caused it to happen to me" (Genesis 27:20). From our perspective, he was taking the Lord's name in vain, lying in the name of God!

Jacob must have gone rigid when his father told him to come close so he could ascertain whether he really was Esau. When Isaac touched Jacob's arms and neck, he was fooled by the goat hair, but the voice was Jacob's. When he asked Jacob if he was Esau. Jacob again lied to his father. Somehow the old man was persuaded. He asked for the meal and afterward pronounced the first-born blessing over Jacob. His final act was to give Jacob a kiss. Rebekah's idea of using Esau's clothes was the right one–the distinctive smell of the outdoors sealed the deal. The text reads:

> So he came close and kissed him; and when he smelled the smell of his garments, he blessed him and said, "See, the smell of my son is like the smell of a field which the Lord has blessed; now may God give you of the dew of heaven, and of the fatness of the earth, and an abundance of grain and new wine; may peoples serve you, and nations bow down to you; be master of your brothers, and may your mother's sons bow down to you. Cursed be those who curse you, and blessed be those who bless you" (Genesis 27:27-29).

What a contradictory scene! It was a sacred time in the presence of God. Both Isaac and Rebekah realized that God Himself was going to be present (27:7), but deception was in the air! Jacob, not Esau, stood before his father as the inheritor of the promise to Abraham. No doubt Jacob had ambivalent and sleazy feelings, but apparently he was convinced, along with his mother, that he was doing what was necessary. After all, God promised him the blessing before he was born!

It is important to note that neither Rebekah nor Jacob (or Isaac for that matter) are *ever* criticized in this story. The entire scene is one of deceit. Yet, *the will of God is accomplished without any of the three incurring blame for their actions.* Great epic literature, whether in the Bible or elsewhere, generally omits moralistic pronouncements. Jacob bargained for the birthright and, with Rebekah, cheated for the blessing and would soon be launched into a series of crises and heartbreaks.

**Finally**

Jacob's two decisions put him on the freeway of his life. His destiny was set. He had made his *big move*, and there was no turning back.

Then as now, it is not so much where you *are*, but where you are heading. It is not so much where you *start* but where you *end*. We are not to place the finish line at the starting point. We must not draw final conclusions about Jacob's life (or ours) at the place where God starts with us. Thankfully many of us can say, "What I've been, I'm not now. What I am now, I will not be in the future." However, each of us needs to ask, "Am I traveling toward the destination in which I will fulfill the purpose for my life, even though my actions may still be flawed?"

THE LEADER'S JOURNEY . . .
**Making your move onto the freeway of life**

Questions for Reflection (alone or in a group):

1.  Do you think Jacob was making a mistake in these two incidents of the birthright and the blessing, or was he justifiably responding to his destiny in this ancient setting and very different culture?

2.  Even though your life may have at times been ugly or messy (like Jacob's), are you on a journey with God now?

3.  What were a couple of the decisions that were important in putting you on the right road for your life?

4.  Are you reasonably sure you are cooperating with the plan God has designed for your life? Are you on the freeway that is leading to your destination and destiny?

**Response**

Praise for God's providence in the decisions that led you to where you are now, and grace to make any course corrections.

# CHAPTER 5

# YOUR BLESSING –
# DON'T DO LIFE WITHOUT IT

＋＝＋

*He who does not have a past, does not have a future.*
*If you have neither a past nor a future, you have no present.*
*John Hannah*

*So Isaac called Jacob and blessed him and charged him,*
*and said to him, "You must not take a wife from the daugh-*
*ters of Canaan."*

*"May God Almighty bless you and make you fruitful and*
*multiply you, that you may become a company of peoples.*

*May He also give you the blessing of Abraham, to you and*
*to your descendants with you, that you may possess the land*
*of your sojournings, which God gave to Abraham!"*

*Now Esau saw that Isaac had blessed Jacob and sent him*
*away to Paddan-aram, to take to himself a wife from there,*
*and that when he blessed him he charged him . . .*
*Genesis 28:1,3,4,6*

*We are . . . supernaturally created for a supernatural work which is supernaturally prepared and is to be supernaturally performed.*

*L. L. Legters*

# YOUR BLESSING –
# DON'T DO LIFE WITHOUT IT

"Is it in you?" A TV commercial shows superb athletes perspiring the bright colors of Gatorade after a grueling competition. They have the magic formula in them. But what we are addressing in this chapter is far more important to a leader than Gatorade is to an athlete. Do you as a leader "have it in you?" Do you have in you the *blessing* necessary to maximize your gifts, abilities and experience?

Jacob's early life reminds us that there is a plan for our lives. What's more, we have an internal architecture for living out our unique plan. We are shaped in our early years and, in time, we make the moves that put us on the freeway of our lives. Subsequent years give us the opportunity to cooperate with God in seeing His plan work in and through our lives.

Now we come to a critical juncture in Jacob's experience. Just before embarking on his journey for the rest of his life, Jacob was blessed by his father. That he got the blessing by deception is no longer an issue. Converted Muslim Ergun Caner speaks of meeting his father seventeen years after he disowned him because he embraced the claims of Jesus Christ. "In our culture, it is an important rite of passage to lay your son in your father's hands" (p. 19). The quest to gain the touch and blessing for an infant son from a father overrode the reality of a broken relationship that was never restored. Similarly, the difficulties between Isaac and Jacob gave way to the blessing that pointed forward to the rest of Jacob's life.

It is more than an ancient custom that is still practiced as a rite in Middle Eastern cultures today. The *blessing factor* is a necessary part of our human development and a rite of passage. *Do we have what is necessary to live the life and fulfill the destiny to which we are called?*

## The *Blessing* Factor

Genesis 27–28 records the events surrounding Jacob's departure from home. In these two chapters, some form of the Hebrew word for *blessing* is used more than twenty-five times. The blessing was concentrated and formalized with Isaac's pronouncement that Jacob was the sole recipient of the covenant entrusted to Abraham. This was no small matter! God had promised Abraham that through his family "all the families of the earth would be blessed." Now Isaac was telling Jacob that *he* was the conduit of the covenant blessing, the one through whom the blessings would come to all the world. *He* was the one who had a special future.

Gary Smalley and John Trent, in their superb book *The Gift of the Blessing,* develop the implications of Jacob's blessing from his father. Their thesis is that a deeply affirming blessing from parents or some other significant person is crucial in one's development. Though neither author received such a blessing from his father, both were blessed in a deep and significant way by other men. Smalley and Trent identify five elements in the blessing of Jacob.

1. Meaningful touch
2. A spoken message
3. Attaching "high value" to the one being blessed
4. Picturing a special future for the one being blessed
5. An active commitment to fulfill the blessing (p.19).

These five principles are repeated in one form or other throughout the Old as well as the New Testament. *Meaningful touch*, be it kissing or embracing or placing a hand on one's head, always accompanied the launching of someone into a special phase of life. As part of the blessing, Isaac asked Jacob to come and kiss him. Two thousand years later, Paul called Timothy to a renewed sense of his ministry by reminding him of the time he received a special and official "laying on of hands" from the Apostle. Warmth, affirmation, acceptance and connectedness are communicated by *touch* in the blessing. The touch and message of blessing go together. The Apostle Paul himself was no stranger to this procedure. When he was smashed to the ground, blinded, called and commissioned on the road to Damascus, nothing happened further until Ananias was sent to tenderly lay hands on him, to call the terrible enemy of the church his brother, and to speak the confirming message to him. God does not do His work in a vacuum of human relationships.

A *spoken message* is the second aspect of blessing. Something has to be spoken into the life of the one being blessed. In this way, *high value* is attached to the one being blessed and a *special future* is delineated. An *active commitment* between the one giving and the one receiving brings closure to the blessing. Each of these elements is found in the words and actions of Isaac toward his son before and after the blessing.

> Then his father Isaac said to him, "Please come close and kiss me, my son." So he came close and kissed him...
>
> So Isaac called Jacob and blessed him . . . May God Almighty bless you and make you fruitful and multiply you, that you may become a company of peoples. May He also give you the blessing of Abraham, to you and to your descendants with you; that you may possess the land of your sojournings, which God gave to Abraham (Genesis 27:26-27; 28:1, 3-4).

Isaac specified God as the Guarantor of the blessing he was conveying to his son. This blessing of Jacob is more than a sentimental story. It is a necessary paradigm for life. Every human being, including the one called to lead others, should be able to say, "I have it in me for I have been blessed by someone who really matters to me." Ronald Rolheiser, in his book *Against an Infinite Horizon*, demonstrates the need each of us has for blessing. His second chapter begins with a quote from Dietrich Bonhoeffer: "A blessing is the visible, perceptible, effective proximity of God" (p. 30). This is exactly what happened to Jacob. His father gave human ratification to a divine reality! Rolheiser notes how "the heart is set free by blessing from our 'elders'" (p. 44).

Blessing nourishes one of the soul's deepest hungers. When blessed, we connect at a deeper level with the reality of being a very special person who has a unique role in life. We are somehow freer to accept God's delight and pleasure in us.

**Father, Bless Me!**

After reading the story of Jacob's blessing and coming to realize how important it is in the life of a leader, I found myself asking business leaders about their own blessing experience. I was attempting to understand the significance of their *blessing factor*. We approached this through a few questions:

1. Did someone to whom you felt especially close ever affirm you as a valuable person who had a special future?
2. If so, what impact did this confirmation have on your life and career?
3. Did this happen before or after you left home?
4. Did it occur on one occasion or over a period of time?

Gavin grew up in a fairly normal home on the eastern seaboard where his father was a passive presence. He talked briefly about his mother's influence, but focused on a journalism professor who communicated clearly that he thought Gavin could be successful as a reporter. He began his career as a sports reporter and today he owns a publishing business! It is exactly what he is fitted and motivated to do! The professor went beyond his class material to play the role of a *seer*. His *blessing* impacted Gavin's life in a powerful and almost predictable way.

Clayton came from a home with a very supportive mother and an unusually successful father who began a company later in his career. "My dad was not a big affirmer, but I remember one special time when he said I was one of the best tool designers he ever met in our product line. I always remembered this when I had a particularly difficult problem." Under Clayton's leadership, the company founded by his father and uncle grew more than twenty times into a business worth millions of dollars. Clayton used the technical skill his father identified and the relational dimension from his mother to find extraordinary blessing as a standout CEO.

Both Gavin and Clayton can identify a significant person who helped launch them into their professional lives. I have shared in each of their lives personally, professionally and spiritually. One of them ends each of our meetings with a hug. It fits! In fact, it is striking to me how their lives so clearly project the blessings they experienced. While both have clear God-given abilities, the blessings from persons they admired profoundly marked what they would do and what they would become.

**Better Late Than Never**

The stories of Gavin, Clayton and many others have caused me to think again about my own *blessing factor*. I received great benefit from parents who were unusually devoted to being what they could and should be to my

75

brother and me. However, I did not take in the complete blessing package that was required for my life before I left home. Two sets of spiritual parents warmly affirmed me and conveyed a deeply felt reality regarding my value as a young man who was beginning a life with God. A lifelong friend of ours saw deeply into my soul and confirmed the fact that my essential contribution and motivational package was building into people's lives. I resisted this for years since I wanted to be an up-front leader. I understand now that her blessing was a release to my truest vocation. Her blessing said essentially, "Charles, how you are wired is not only okay, it is wonderful!"

One thing especially left me feeling a little empty–it was a lack of the *special touch* that Trent and Smalley identify as the first element in Jacob's blessing. This is why I look back gratefully to an instance when several leaders took initiative to lay their hands on my head and shoulders when we were launching *Life Serve*. Now I know this commissioning is a part of my blessing package.

## Blessing in a Broken World

We are speaking of the blessing factor in our modern world where intergenerational continuity, as well as deeply bonded relationships in the family or an inner circle, is so often impaired or lacking. Many people just *don't have it when they leave home.*

A woman told me with deep sadness that her father never once took her on his lap and told her he loved her, let alone expressed what a special and extraordinary person she was. Her father stole her blessing!

What does a person do when the special blessing was never conveyed? We need to know that God is always bigger than the models or paradigms. He is the ultimate reality and stands above the norms that operate generally. Our very lack of blessing can become part of our equipping.

Colin is a powerful example of this and his story points us in the right direction. He is a model husband and father. He attempts to live a balanced life, and this includes having a beautiful cabin in the north woods of Wisconsin where he and his family retreat for times together. As a well-paid executive, he is esteemed as a critical player in a large family-owned business and has gained a national reputation in his industry. He also is committed to serving men who carry wounds that are holding them back. He is a leader in intensive weekend "marathons" devoted to helping these men find the healing they seek.

Colin's unusually strong business ability can be traced back to his father who was president of a company which was always in an enviable financial position. However, Colin paid a high price for a similar gift. His father was somewhat abusive and emotionally detached from his family. He was living out a dismal two-generation inheritance.

Colin's father often went to his room after work, ate alone and lived a darkly depressed life. He never had much time for his children. As a result, Colin left home with some severe problems. Damaged and dysfunctional, he carried the heritage of a broken life with him, became a college dropout and was plagued with alcoholism.

After years of minimal emotional connection with his father, Colin's father developed a terminal heart condition and experienced a spiritual renewal. He began communicating with Colin as never before. When his condition reached a critical point, Colin and his family traveled to North Carolina from Chicago for what they thought was a final visit.

During this special weekend. Colin's father decided to tell his story. Because of his failing health, he was only able to get up to age eleven of his pain-filled life this first day. It took several more hours to finish his personal narrative the next day. Along with telling the events of his life, his father was able to bless his son. The blessing and bonding between father and son culminated with a picture in which Colin's emaciated father put his arm around Colin, looking lovingly and deeply into his son's eyes. It was thirty years late, but Colin got his needed blessing!

How is it that part of Colin's equipping today stems from his lack of blessing earlier in his life? Colin's tormented life eventually led him to Alcoholics Anonymous and on to the famous Willow Creek Church in the northwest suburbs of Chicago where he experienced a personal relationship with Jesus Christ followed by extensive counseling. It was out of this past that he was launched into a special journey with God. It was also from this background that he became the husband and father his own father was unable to be. Coming directly out of his own troubled life passage is his sought-after ability to be a leader of men who want the life with God and the wholeness out of brokenness he has found. His lack of blessing from his father helped to drive him to the total blessing package he has today.

**James**

We speak to one final issue using James' experience. James is one of the company presidents we noted in chapter 2 who took his father's company and his own career to a level way beyond his father's ability. Since he was mentored into his business career from boyhood up, I thought I knew how he would answer the questions, but I was wrong. When asked if he had ever received a special affirmation from a significant person, he could not remember any person who had affirmed him.

He responded to my questions by saying, "I am an independent dude who has had to fight his way through life without any help from anybody. I have had to figure out everything myself. Neither of my parents was available to help me." He came to his father once when the company was in deep trouble and looked like it might need a financial infusion. His dad told him he was on his own! I pushed a little further to try to find some *blessing factor* that was significant from growing up in the business. "I observed my father's mistakes and learned how not to repeat the way he did these things." Case closed! That was it, I couldn't get any positive response about his father or any other mentor, although James is very familiar with the idea that "everybody has to have a mentor." He concluded by saying, "It was just God and me."

If you are like James who has gained unusual success but feels no one's touch or affirmation in a blessing role, how about looking into your heart at this time? When you let down your defenses, do you feel a certain sadness, anger or resentment? Do you live with an underlying sense of isolation or disconnectedness in most of your relationships? Do you have trouble letting anyone touch your life in a meaningful way? Could you receive warm affirmation in a significant relationship that would impact you in an unprecedented way, or would you be emotionally bound to reject it because of the pain that might surface?

The big issue is whether or not you are equipped with what you need to fulfill the plan for your life and meet your destiny, now that you have turned on to the freeway of your life. You may feel that some necessary component of your life is missing. Remember that the Bible is a book of blessing, and God is the God of blessing. Some form of the word *blessing* is found more than 500 times in the Bible. Perhaps you feel a need to pray like Jabez did in the Old Testament, "Oh, that You would bless me and extend my border" (1 Chronicles 4:10). The answer to his prayer is that "God granted him his request!" Like Jabez and Jacob, don't settle for anything less than the blessing required for your life.

Have you permitted yourself a *gut check* with respect to your blessing? Do you have *the blessing?* Blessing occurs when someone with whom you are warmly connected or bonded affirms your great value and points to your special future. In this way, a human being is confirming or affirming the divine reality that is stamped on your life. Do you have it in you? If you don't, what is keeping you from asking for it or building a relationship with people who may be able to see deeply into your life and affirm what they see there? Jacob didn't stop until he had it all. Why should you?

THE LEADER'S JOURNEY . . .

**Receiving *the blessing* from someone with whom you are closely connected who cooperates with the reality that God already has determined by deeply affirming your value and your special future**

Questions for Reflection (alone or in a group):

1. What impacted you the most from this chapter?

2. Has someone with whom you are closely connected affirmed your great value and pointed toward your special future?

3. Do you feel anything is missing in terms of being blessed like Jacob was or in the manner we described the modern-day process?

4. Have you received the *blessing* required for you to live out the purpose or plan for your life? Do you have any idea what that purpose is?

5. Would it be helpful to talk to a resource person to sort through any issues that have surfaced for you?

**Response**

Praise for those who have contributed special blessings that have become an important part of your life package.

# CHAPTER 6

# THE LEADER'S JOURNEY TO BETHEL –
# JACOB'S CONTINENTAL DIVIDE

*It is a commonplace of all religious thought,
even the most primitive,
that the man seeking visions and insight must
go apart from his fellows
and live for a time in the wilderness.*

*Loren Eisely*

*Then Jacob departed from Beersheba and went toward
Haran. He came to a certain place and spent the night
there, because the sun had set; and he took one of the stones
of the place and put it under his head, and lay down in that
place. He had a dream, and behold, a ladder was set on the
earth with its top reaching to heaven; and behold, the
angels of God were ascending and descending on it. And
behold, the LORD stood above it and said, "I am the LORD,
the God of your father Abraham and the God of Isaac."*

*Genesis 28:10-13a*

*But when God, who had set me apart even*
*from my mother's womb*
*and called me through His grace, was pleased*
*to reveal His Son in me . . .*
*I did not immediately consult with flesh and blood . . .*
*but I went away to Arabia.*

*Galatians 1:15-17*

*Consequently, King Agrippa, I did not prove disobedient to the heavenly vision.*

*Acts 26:19*

# THE LEADER'S JOURNEY TO BETHEL – JACOB'S CONTINENTAL DIVIDE

Can you point to an incident in your past that resulted in a monumental change in how you lived? Have you had an experience so dramatic that you think in *before and after* terms? Was there ever an event that seemed to set the direction and tone for the rest of your life? If so, you have experienced a "continental divide" event much like Jacob had at Bethel. In this chapter we will look at the continental divide principle in the life of a leader. Recognizing and reflecting on your experience may help catapult you into a new level of life and leadership.

## To Bethel via Catalina Island

My personal struggle to somehow get in contact with God was highlighted one night during my senior year in high school when my brother and I slept outdoors. When I looked up at the brilliant array of stars, my mind was swirling out of control as I tried to believe in a God who was able to create such an immeasurable universe. I finally fell to sleep, still unable to believe in a God who felt so distant.

A few weeks later, as I was painting the east side of our home, my mother stuck her head out the door and yelled, "Charles, you've got a phone call." Hurrying to the phone, I listened to a businessman in our church who suggested that I attend the InterVarsity camp on Catalina Island twenty-seven miles off the coast of Los Angeles! "Thanks, Mr. Ostle, but I don't believe I have the money." But after two days on a Greyhound bus from St. Louis, a night in an equipment box on the end of a peer in Avalon Harbor after missing the boat to the island, I was at the camp!

While sharing this time with college students from around the country, I became increasingly uneasy. I lacked the personal relationship with God that many of them expressed so naturally. At the time, there was no way I could have known I hadn't gone to California simply to attend a camp. This was preparing me for a "continental divide" experience that changed my life forever! Here is what took place.

After my time at camp was over, I accompanied a group of student leaders to the Klamath Falls area of Oregon to serve a rural church while the pastor vacationed. Within a couple days of our arrival, I began a smothering descent into personal darkness. By the middle of the week, I was so utterly downcast that someone asked, "What is wrong with you?" Before I could fade into the background or bolt out of the room, the words jumped out of my lips, "I don't know Jesus Christ." With that I ran to the church sanctuary and waited . . . through the morning . . . through lunch and into the afternoon.

That afternoon, something happened that radically changed and refocused my life. I didn't see an angel or hear a voice (every member of the group wisely left me alone). I didn't even pray. But on that day in my solitary and even angry confrontation with God, something quietly transpired in my soul. I crossed my personal continental divide! There was a new and permanent reality for me in which I could truly say from my heart, "I can know God and I do know God."

**Jacob's Journey to a Certain Place**

Familiar landmarks passed from sight as Jacob fled from his home for Syria. Anyone in his situation would have questions. "What's going to happen to me? How long will I be away from home? Is God going to judge me for what I did to my brother? Will there be a woman to marry in Uncle Laban's family?" Surely he was scared of the unknown. Many people have felt that "Old Jake was getting what he deserved when he took it on the lam to run away from Esau." Even his mother noted that Esau was after him because of "what you did to him" (Genesis 28:45), although it was her plan in the first place!

One evening while he trekked, "he came to a certain place and spent the night there, because the sun had set" (28:11). The Hebrew word for "place" is used six times in the passage to indicate subtle attention to this barren, unpromising, and apparently random scene. The reader knows something is about to happen to Jacob at this certain spot in the desert, but Jacob had no way of knowing what it would become for him. There was no way to predict that this would become one of the great night experiences of the Bible (ranking with David at Adullam, Ruth at the threshing floor, and Nicodemus' conversation with Jesus).

Jacob's immediate concerns for the night related to water and food, safety, and whatever comfort he could gain from a night of rest. His outer garment protected him from the heat of the long day but was hardly sufficient for the cold of the desert night. Even so, sleep was a welcome respite from fatigue and as an insulator from the questions swirling in his head.

If you were asked about the most sacred moment of your life or the event producing the most lasting effect, what comes to mind? Jacob was about to gain an answer to this question on this night in a certain place in the desert.

## Jacob's Dream

After Jacob settled in for the night and dropped off to sleep with a rock for a pillow, he had a dream. Dreams are always important in the Old Testament, but this one is particularly striking in that there are three "beholds" that describe the dream. H.C. Leupold, an Old Testament scholar, sees this event vividly when he writes, "The surprise occasioned by the character of the dream is reflected by the threefold *hinneh*–'behold': behold a ladder, angels, and Yahweh." The idea is that the reader should stop, look, and listen carefully because something dramatic is about to happen. Simply put, God intruded unexpectedly during Jacob's unguarded moments of sleep.

The nature of this divine encounter was important. Jacob was not totally free from the stress of his escape. Had an angel been hurtling toward him or the awesome light of the glory of God been the subject of his dream, Jacob would most likely have had a fear-flight reaction. His already burdened nervous system would have been overloaded! Instead, the *first* image of the dream was a ladder "set on the earth with its top reaching to heaven" (Genesis 28:12). Jacob immediately perceived this as a friendly overture of contact rather than aggression. But what kind of ladder could reach from earth to heaven?

It was not a modern extension ladder flexing precariously under its otherworldly traffic! The use of the word "ladder" in other sources leads scholars to believe that Jacob saw huge slabs of limestone laid on top of each other so as to form a massive staircase. People from Ur in Lower Mesopotamia, Abraham's point of emigration, identified such a ladder as a ziggurat stair. Ziggurats were enormous buildings like rectangular pyramids with external steps. Each of the three stories was set back from the other and the third story contained a shrine for the deity of the city and "was known in the Sumerian ritual as 'heaven.' . . . During the long journey undertaken by Abraham with his clan, going up the valley of the Euphrates, from Ur to Haran, the Hebrew shepherds would have been able to see a number of these high towers in the distance" (Epp, p. 144). That a divine message would be communicated in familiar images is confirmed by F.B. Meyer when he writes, "The Spirit of God always conveyed His teachings to His servant in language borrowed from their surroundings" (pp. 11, 34).

On the enormous staircase we find the *second* startling feature of Jacob's dream. "Behold, angels were ascending and descending on the ladder" (28:12). What seems to be stressed here is not the fact that there were angels on the steps, but rather the order of the angelic movement. They were first ascending and then descending. They weren't coming to *get* Jacob. The dream made it clear that God's angels were already *with* Jacob, perhaps guarding and guiding him. God truly cared about this fugitive. For someone on the run, this is important!

The *third* crucial feature of the dream happened at the top of the staircase. "Behold, at the top of the ladder stood the Lord" (28:13). From this vantage point God spoke comforting words to Jacob, confirming the promise that had been made concerning him before his birth. The God of his grandfather, Abraham, and father, Isaac, made it clear that Jacob was the one through whom the covenant would be kept.

**What Leaders Need When They Are on the Run**

Leaders often feel out of contact and isolated, friendless and without anyone who really understands them. After all, "It's lonely at the top!" Jacob knew the feeling. He was now unplugged from all that he had known and not yet connected to his new home. He was uncertain how his future would unfold. There was no one in the desert who could truly empathize with him. That is why the ladder vision was so powerful and necessary.

The ladder was a point of *contact* to a disconnected person! The staircase was a symbol of divine connection. While Jacob felt alienated from his home and family, God made sure Jacob knew that he was not alone. Yet Jacob needed more than a point of contact. He needed *companionship*, and he found to his great surprise that this lone spot was populated. It was "*the gate of heaven*," and the angels were his companions.

But Jacob had another, even more compelling need. He needed *compassion*. Probably feeling like a liar and thief, Jacob needed someone to show him unconditional love. The vision of the ladder, with the promises offered by the One standing at the top, made it clear that he was loved. Leaders also need someone who can say, "I care about you. I am concerned for you. Even though you have failed, I will always look for the best in you. I love you and will stick up for you. I am still going to keep my promises to you."

## The Last Eighteen Inches of God's Journey
## to Jacob's Heart

Moderns sometimes try to live "without the ladder." It doesn't matter how sophisticated the culture, brilliant the technology, or liberated the people are. Whenever God's ladder is lost so that people have no prospect of being able to personally encounter God, they eventually drift to despair, meaninglessness, suicide, or irrational acts.

God was determined to keep Jacob from drifting! To do that meant building a ladder that would span not only the great distance from earth to heaven, but also the distance from Jacob's head to his heart. It was through the ladder vision that God bridged the final eighteen inches between Jacob's heart and head. When God crossed this bridge by linking Himself to Abraham and Isaac, He established a deeply felt commonality with Jacob. This connection was the way to Jacob's heart. This "certain place" became Jacob's "continental divide" experience. He was forever changed. In the morning he honored what had happened by naming the place *Bethel*, literally, "the house of God."

## New Bethels without Ladders

Bethel experiences come in many places. Zacchaeus was in a tree. Little Samuel was lying on his bed in the Tabernacle. Martin Luther was wasting away in his monk's cell. What turned out to be a Bethel experience for Nicodemus began with a nighttime visit to Jesus where he learned he must be born again. Paul was traveling to Damascus under the name of Saul. But no matter what the circumstances, the Bethel experience is always one in which there is a *revelation* of God which results in a personal *relationship* with God.

A unique encounter with God is exactly what happened to a young West Point cadet some years ago. Unfortunately, he had written some bad checks and was spending time in jail. A businessman turned chaplain came by one day to preach while this young man was playing cards. It was an unlikely place for a Bethel experience, but that is exactly what happened to the cadet. He crossed his continental divide. Years later the former cadet had become president of a prison ministry and was featured in a film. The set included the very cellblock where he was converted. The West Point graduate traced his success to his jail cell! His "certain place" did not include a ladder, but it was just as much a "Bethel" experience as Jacob had.

**Finally**

Do you recall how God made contact with you and reached you at the deepest level of your personality and identity? How did He bridge the gap to you making Himself known in such a way that your life was refocused? Perhaps you are realizing that this has never happened to you. If God took the initiative with Jacob, surely He will respond if you venture out to Him and perhaps take a further step of finding someone who knows the reality you are seeking. For you to arrive at your own Bethel, because you spent time with Jacob, would be unbelievably special!

THE LEADER'S JOURNEY . . .
**Meeting God in a transforming experience
that refocuses life around a new reality
and relationship**

Questions for Reflection (alone or in a group):

1.  How might Jacob's life have been changed after his Bethel encounter as he continued the journey to his uncle's home in Syria?

2.  Describe your personal continental divide or a life experience that altered the direction of your life and what changes followed.

3.  Do you recall observing the changes in someone who experienced a life-altering experience with God like Jacob did at Bethel?

4.  After considering Jacob's experience, do you find yourself wanting something more in your life? Is there something you need to do about this?

**Response**

Worship for the way in which God has intersected your life making it possible for you to know Him personally. (Prayer for this reality if you have yet to experience it.)

# CHAPTER 7

# BETHEL POSTSCRIPT –
# FINDING YOUR PERSONAL
# UNIVERSE
# IN YOUR LIFE PACKAGE

*If we are to make ultimate sense of our lives,
all the disparate elements in us have to be integrated
around call.*

*Elizabeth O'Connor*

*And behold, the LORD stood above it and said, "I am the
LORD, the God of your father Abraham and the God of
Isaac; the land on which you lie, I will give it to you and to
your descendants. Your descendants will also be like the
dust of the earth, and you will spread out to the west and to
the east and to the north and to the south; and in you and in
your descendants shall all the families of the earth be
blessed. Behold, I am with you and will keep you wherever
go, and will bring you back to this land; for I will not leave
you until I have done what I have promised you."*

*Genesis 28:13-15*

*We are half-hearted creatures, fooling about*
*with drink and sex and ambition*
*when infinite joy is offered us, like an ignorant child*
*who wants to go on*
*making mud pies in a slum because he cannot imagine*
*what is meant by the offer of a holiday at the sea.*
*We are far too easily pleased.*

*C.S. Lewis*

# BETHEL POSTSCRIPT –
# FINDING YOUR PERSONAL UNIVERSE
# IN YOUR LIFE PACKAGE

A re you okay with your life? Is your life package as big as you would like it to be? Are the boundaries around your life too small? Is the company, organization or church big enough, influential enough, or good enough as a platform for your leadership abilities? Do you need more? Have you established parameters or borders to frame your life?

While we will look at career concerns later, we return to Jacob's experience at Bethel to explore a more basic issue. Careers are critical but they don't necessarily satisfy, because they are external. In this chapter we are looking at our personal universe, or how our lives might be packaged.

Think about two leaders who achieved enviable success and gained freedom to do almost anything they wanted. Lea Fastow, from one of the leading families of Houston, proved that a woman can rise to the highest levels of a major corporation. Her success story was the subject of various articles, but it didn't last. She found herself reporting to a federal detention center where she shared "an 8-foot-by-10-foot cell in a gray, 11-story building where the only chance to go outside is during brief and rare outings on the roof. She'll probably work preparing food or doing laundry for 50 cents a day" (*Daily Herald*).

What happened? Lea joined with her husband in the activities that led to the collapse of Enron and its $30 billion loss of stock value. She and her husband are attempting to have their penitentiary sentences run separately so that one will be available to their two young children while the other serves time.

Bernard Ebbers rose even more spectacularly from a career as a milkman to become CEO of WorldCom, a major telecommunications firm. He was charged with orchestrating an $11 billion fraudulent scheme including a guarantee from the business for $400 million of personal loans. He was found guilty on all counts and, as a sixty-three-year-old man, faces a possible sentence of eighty-five years (*Daily Herald*).

The headline of one of the articles read, "Ebbers Ignored Roots." That is the issue. We have roots that we should not ignore, life boundaries that we can't afford to disregard. A life without boundaries is a life in trouble. Since a leadership role gives people a larger than average playing field, leaders are often tempted to play out of bounds personally and professionally–famous one day and infamous the next–moving quickly from triumph to tragedy, living high and ending low, demanding respect and earning disrepute.

**Stay in the Box**

Thomas was moving in a much different direction. As we met on the deck of his beautiful home, he surfaced a concern. On the eve of his fortieth birthday, he owned a premier restaurant with his brother, and his leadership was in demand. He and his wife were invited to be palace guests by the President of Cyprus while staying in their summer home on the island. He had gained a reputation as one of the outstanding young evangelical Greek leaders in the U.S. and abroad.

His eyes were searching and earnest as he asked, "What now? Do I have to experience more of the same to be successful? Do I have to climb higher on the success ladder?" Realizing the struggle in his soul, I weighed my answers very carefully. It was Jacob's experience at Bethel that helped me provide a framework for Thomas. I used the analogy of a *life box*–the context or circumstances where we live.

All of us live within boundaries. Our culture, circumstances, backgrounds, limitations or abilities place us all within some kind of life parameters. The opportunities we have come in some kind of package. This is where we are to find our personal universe. Before we look at the life package God entrusted to Jacob at Bethel, let's see how we worked on it with Thomas.

"Thomas, your life package is like a box that will not only provide you with protection from foolish or shattering failure, but will also give you a life that is full and without regret. The first side of your *life box* is **personal relationships.** The relationships that surround you offer the support you need and more than that, provide a place or platform where you are to serve at the highest level, make the greatest impact and experience the fullest life.

"Think about it. You, your wife and children are looked up to–people want what you have. You have special responsibility with your divorced mother, your brother and extended family members, some of whom you helped begin their own businesses which are now established and successful.

"You have almost 100 employees–some of them single moms–that make up a group larger than many church congregations. You are important in the restaurant business and have influence with scores of restaurant owners. You are a recognized leader in the Cypriot community with instant respect that a missionary would take years to earn. You are loved and respected by Greek leaders and Christians here and abroad. You have leadership responsibilities and opportunities in numerous other venues as well.

"You have an untarnished reputation and, as you know, 'A good name is to be more desired than great riches, favor is better than silver and gold' (Proverbs 22:1). Violating any of your relational trusts would carry a very high cost.

"For you to descend to any self-serving, morally questionable or base relationship catering to your short-term interests is out of the question. The personal relational aspect of your *life box* is where you are to invest. Stay true to your **personal relationships.**

"Thomas, the next side of the box holds everything else

together and gives meaning to the whole. If we took a box and turned it on its side, we would put this side down as the support for the whole. This life parameter is your **relationship with God**.

"Several years ago, when a pastor challenged you to a relationship with God, the reality, direction and content of your life dramatically changed. A phrase on a T-shirt I saw pretty well sums it up, 'Man's mind stretched to a new idea never goes back to its original dimension.' The presence of God is the reality and dimension that shapes and drives your life. You are to live into this **relationship** with God the rest of your life, and it will take that long. If your life runs on these two tracks of faithfulness to the **relationships** entrusted to you, you will be well on your way to reaching your full potential."

The morning was giving way to lunch time. I needed to finish the life-box analogy so that he would have whatever he needed for the challenges he faced. "Thomas, if your **personal relationships** and your **relationship with God** are the boundaries of your life that keep you from the worst and keep you on target for the best, you also need to look at the **plan** that drives you.

"You have come to realize that God has determined a **plan** for your life that is so good, so big and so important that you should be compelled to pursue it the rest of your years. This **plan** will drive you. You understand that it involves the ministries where you play a role. You are succeeding when you follow the **plan** as a devoted husband and father. You understand that your position as a successful restaurateur is the platform on which you stand in your community and circles of influence. Diligence is required here and is nonnegotiable. Thomas, follow the **plan**. Explore it. Live it out. Don't deviate. God is not hiding it, but leading you in it step by step. Follow the **plan!**"

One more side of the box remained. "Thomas, sometimes we settle into the terrific realities of life and get complacent. We need something to pull us along or move us beyond generalities to the specifics. A good basketball player can be great only by working on the specifics of his game–free throws, jump shots, lay-ups, fast breaks, passing or shots in the paint.

"The fourth side of the box that will help pull you along are the **goals** you set. Sometimes the **plan** can get a little hazy or seem to lack substance. **Goals** help pull you along because they add specifics, are defined and keep you reaching. For example, you might better define your desire to know God more intimately by changing your routine of study or personal devotions, going on a personal retreat, memorizing a few verses, or deciding to use the accountability that a group brings. You might translate your desire for a stronger marriage into measurable activities such as setting aside time to communicate when you disagree, committing to regular date nights, or making sure you take time to select the right gifts for special occasions.

"Whatever needs adjusting in your life can be translated into **goals** that will keep you on track. The box is complete with **goals,** which are often measurable and practical expressions of the other three sides of your *life box.* Your **goals** should be the tangible expressions of the deepest realities of your life."

Our time was up. Thomas's tears indicated that he signed on with heart and mind. Ever since that time when Thomas mentions "staying in the box," we each know what he means! At Bethel, Jacob confronted similar principles and, like Thomas, signed on to them with his entire being.

### Bethel: Jacob's Life Package

When Jacob lay down to sleep on a rock pillow in a land which he didn't own, he had no way of anticipating what he would learn that night through his dream vision. God's plan was so big that God gave him a whole land, an entire nation, to accommodate the **plan** for him. However, He didn't start there. Jacob's *life package* was established first with a **relationship**. God gave Jacob a relationship with Himself before He gave him the **plan** for his life.

This **relationship** was the reality which welded his *life box* together and became Jacob's personal universe–entirely big enough for the rest of his life. When Jacob dreamed his vision dream, it was the LORD, the self-revealing God above the ladder, who identified Himself by making the connection to lonely Jacob's father and grandfather.

What impressed Jacob more than anything else was the absolute reality of God in his dream vision. When the sun rose on Jacob's sleeping figure the next morning, the burning reality from the night before was now a part of his deepest being. "It was the LORD I encountered last night! The LORD is in this place! It's God's house! It's the gate of heaven!" (Genesis 28:16-17) He could live *in* and *out* of this reality the rest of his life–and he did!

This is what business leaders need to know. You can't live in the reality of $50 million, a large business, or national prominence. As real and alluring as these things are, what sustains life is nowhere to be found in them. Jacob's *life package* and fundamental reality of his life was built first on a **relationship** that God established with him.

The second side of this amazing *life box* was the **plan**. Jacob, who didn't even own the stone he used for a pillow, was informed that the **plan** was so big that it would take an entire land to contain it.

1. God was giving the entire land to Jacob and his descendents.

2. His descendents would be numerous like the desert sand spreading to the east, west, north, and south.

3. His descendents would be fundamental players in God's plan for the world. They were destined to be the

human channel through whom God's greatest blessing for mankind would come.

4. God's **plan** included the "insurance" which he badly needed. Jacob was promised safe passage and preservation through his dangerous life. He spent much of his life living on the edge and ran for his life more than once. The LORD emphasizes the safety theme for His frightened adopted son–perhaps Jacob's greatest felt need at the moment: "I am *with* you . . . will *keep* you . . . will *bring you back* . . . will *not leave* you *until I have done*. . ." (Genesis 28:15).

We sometimes fret over what we don't know about the **plan** for our lives. It helps to be reminded that the basics are already given to us. For example, Romans 8:32 notes that God intends to give us anything and everything that is really good because He didn't spare His own Son to make it all available to us. You can buy into a plan like that!

We see a Bible character like the Apostle Paul wrestling with the specifics of the plan when he traveled to Asia Minor to reach his assigned people group–the Gentiles. He was following the master plan, but was instructed not to invest any further effort where he was (Acts 16:6-12). He was already moving west exactly as he should have been. He just wasn't far enough west. We too need to be sold on the big picture plan and discern the specifics in transit!

The third side of the *life package* is **personal relationships.** In Jacob's life box, they represented the core contribution of his life. It was what he was born to do. His destiny is determined as patriarch, progenitor or founder of an entire nation or people group.

An entire nation carries his name today–the exact fulfillment of God's promise. These people are called the Children of Israel in the Bible. He spent much of his life growing into this name of Israel. The nation is often called Jacob as well!

As we look at the rest of his life, we see it wrapped up in

family and descendants. He never stopped grieving after Rachel died. He never stopped mourning when Joseph was thought to be dead. The very last days of his life included an extended and far-reaching prophetic blessing on his sons and Joseph's two sons–his grandsons.

The final side of Jacob's life box was his response to God's plan with his own set of goals. Here are the **goals** that Jacob had the audacity to ask God to fulfill (Genesis 28:20-28).

1. "Be with me!" Jacob asked God to commit Himself to what He had already promised as a present tense reality (Genesis 28:15).

2. "Keep me!" After reading what God already promised Jacob, we can wonder if he heard or believed what God had already told him. It sounds like us when we are in dangerous territory and wonder if we can trust God.

3. "Feed and clothe me!" God was going to make Jacob "exceedingly prosperous" (Genesis 30:40). Jacob wanted the contract tied down, but he was asking for far less than God was going to provide.

4. "Bring me back safely!" This is key for a frightened young man. Sometimes just surviving can be our most immediate concern.

If God would meet these goals, then Jacob promised some contingency goals in his relationship with God.

1. His first contingent goal commitment was, "You will be my God after You fulfill the contract." (Not, "You are my God whether I live or die.")

2. His second was to make the place where God met him hallowed and recognizably sacred. Are you keeping any sacred or set apart places in your life that are between you and God?

3. His third goal intention was to give God 10 percent off the top. For what he was demanding, doesn't this seem to be a small-minded offer? After what God has done for you and

me, what we give is often not much to brag about either.

Done deal! Jacob then went on his way (Genesis 29:1), but he never forgot. God on His part accepted the brash offer, and eventually called Jacob back to this place that was now sacred to them both. You may not be attracted to Jacob's brashness, but at least he was serious and specific with God, and the Lord seemed okay with that.

## Get Ganas

It is not surprising that the principles from this hallowed incident in Jacob's life are so relevant to leaders today. We could only wish that the CEOs and high-ranking executives who are profiled in their downward spirals in the business pages understood the *paradigm of the box!* A *life box* or *life package* is made up of a supreme **relationship** that is the core reality of life, the **personal relationships** in which we invest our lives, a **plan** that will drive us, and **goals** that specify the plan and help pull us along.

We can find a personal universe as Jacob did that is perfectly suitable for us. We just need to stay in the box and fill in the dimensions of the *life package* with our name on it.

*Reality check:* Do you have a core reality that provides substance for the rest of your life–a **relationship** with God who is Creator, Author of our personhood and Father who brings us to a personal relationship through Jesus Christ?

*Reality check:* Are you investing in the **relationships** where you will make your greatest life contribution, instead of getting involved in counterproductive, short-term self-serving interests?

*Reality check:* Are you driven by a **plan** for your life that keeps you going even when futility seems to be the norm?

*Reality check:* Have you taken time and effort to make sure that your **goals** which *pull* you along are specific, short-term expressions of the big picture you have chosen for your life?

Jerry Campagna in his article, "Faith, Focus and Ganas Propel Us Through Life's Journey," speaks of interviewing more than 100 top Latino leaders in the United States who all had *ganas*, "something like 'a burning fire in the belly to win the race in the midst of overwhelming obstacles!'" If we stay in *the box* and find our *life package*, we will have *ganas*–a burning motivation to stay the course and gain the biggest prize possible for our lives!

THE LEADER'S JOURNEY. . .
> **Understanding that you have a *life package*
> or *box* where you will experience the great-
> est fulfillment, highest achievements and
> become the person you were meant to be.**

Questions for Reflection (alone or in a group):

1. Does the idea of "living in your box to find your personal universe" make sense at this point in your experience?

2. Are you reasonably sure what your *life package* is supposed to be? If not, how might you go about clarifying this critical concern?

3. From your current understanding, describe as best you can what your *life package* is.

4. By finding out how to live in your *life box*, are you finding freedom from possessions that don't provide satisfaction, power without lasting purpose, importance without substance, or achievements that lack significance?

5. Are you jumping over the sides of your *life box* at this time and failing to live into the call or destiny of your life? If so, what measures will you take?

6. To what extent are you committed to living in and working out your **relationship with God**, investing your life in the **personal relationships** entrusted to you, following the **plan** as best you understand it, and working on the **goals** that are the short-term expressions of your *life package*?

## Response

Praise for the adequate life package entrusted to you and prayer that you will live fully in these parameters.

# CHAPTER 8

# CAREER CONCEPTS

╬═╬

*Working with top executives . . . has convinced me that people who get to the top of the ladder seldom ask if it's leaning against the right wall.*

*Larry W. Poland*

*"But now, when shall I provide for my own household also?"*
*So he said, "What shall I give you?"*
*And Jacob said, "You shall not give me anything. If you will do this one thing for me, I will again pasture and keep your flock: let me pass through your entire flock today, removing from there every speckled and spotted sheep, and every black one among the lambs, and the spotted and speckled among the goats; and such shall be my wages.". . . So the man became exceedingly prosperous, and had large flocks and female and male servants and camels and donkeys.*

*Genesis 30:30–32, 43*

*Vocation does not come from willfulness. It comes from listening . . . .*
*The word vocation itself . . . is rooted in the Latin for "voice."*
*Vocation does not mean a goal that I pursue.*
*It means a calling that I hear.*

*Parker Palmer*

# CAREER CONCEPTS

"What is your career?" When I ask this question of successful business leaders, I am particularly interested in their "top of the head" responses. Conner answered, "A somewhat successful investment consultant." Gavin's reply was longer. "I'm a business publisher. Careers have different stages. I was a student, a professional sports writer, a business publisher, editor and now an entrepreneurial business owner." When I called Thomas, he said, "I am disguised as a restauranteur. I am an ambassador for Christ." Wesley's firm serves large companies or organizations in the United States and England. "Marketing and communications" were the words he used.

There is a common element in these answers. Each points to what the leader does. Dictionary definitions of *career* help answer this question. "Pursuing a normally temporary activity as a lifework" highlights the transitory nature of what one does with his or her life. Another definition is "one's advancement or achievement in a particular vocation." The idea of progression, ongoing achievement or dynamic improvement is implicit. Another description of career is "a general course of action, an occupation or calling." What is included in this general course of action? Is this limited to what we do for a living? Does it refer to the major ventures for which we are known (like being a manufacturer, philanthropist and antique car collector)? Looking at Jacob's life may help us see career in a different light.

## Career 101

In Genesis 30:30 we see Jacob wrestling with a very basic question: "But now, when shall I provide for my own household also?" He was exactly where most of us are early in life. "I've got a family to take care of. What is the best way for me to do that?" Jacob understood his career to involve a vocation that would provide for his large family in the most effective way possible. The birth of his eleventh son seemed to be the catalyst for his decision.

For fourteen years Jacob had been working as a hired servant for his father-in-law. It was finally time for Jacob to be his own man. He confronted Laban with the inevitable request.

Now it came about when Rachel had borne Joseph, that Jacob said to Laban, "Send me away, that I may go to my own place and to my own country. Give me my wives and my children for whom I have served you, and let me depart; for you yourself know my service which I have rendered you" (30:25-26).

But because Laban had profited so greatly with Jacob working for him, he was not ready to see his son-in-law leave. To keep Jacob around, Laban told him to "write his own ticket" (30:28). Jacob's big moment had come.

Before naming his price, Jacob reminded Laban of his excellent service the past fourteen years. He reminded him that it was the Lord's intervention through his service that had made Laban a wealthy man (30:29-30). Consequently, Jacob was in a superior bargaining position. He knew this was his chance and he took it. His request focused on animals as working capital.

So he said, "What shall I give you?" And Jacob said, "You shall not give me anything. If you will do this one thing for me, I will again pasture and keep your flock: let me pass through your entire flock today, removing from there every speckled and spotted sheep and every black one among the lambs, and the spotted and speckled among the goats; and such shall be my wages" (30:31-32).

The plan seemed reasonable. The few speckled and spotted animals could easily be identified and given to Jacob. Laban's flocks would only increase in numbers and value after Jacob's few animals were removed. A deal was struck. Laban thought he had the best of both worlds–his daughters and grandchildren weren't leaving and his son-in-law couldn't overtake him in wealth. But that was about to change!

## Genetic Engineering–Divine and Very Human Partners

The strategies Jacob had used to make Laban wealthy became wildly successful when he worked his own business. We read, "The man became exceedingly prosperous, and had large flocks and female and male servants and camels and donkeys" (30:43). But how this happened is stranger than fiction. Here is how it is summarized in the biblical account.

Then Jacob took fresh rods of poplar and almond and plane trees, and peeled white stripes in them, exposing the white which was in the rods. He set the rods which he had peeled in front of the flocks in the gutters, even in the watering troughs, where the flocks came to drink; and they mated when they came to drink. So the flocks mated by the rods, and the flocks brought forth striped, speckled, and spotted. Jacob separated the lambs, and made the flocks face toward the striped and all the black in the flock of Laban; and he put his own herds apart, and did not put them with Laban's flock. Moreover, whenever the stronger of the flock were mating, Jacob would place the rods in the sight of the flock in the gutters, so that they might mate by the rods; but when the flock was feeble, he did not put them in; so the feebler were Laban's and the stronger Jacob's (Genesis 30:37-42).

This visual stimulation for the mating animals resulted in the mutation of their offspring! It was genetic engineering with wooden rods rather than test tubes! How this happened has generated discussion and debate for centuries. One author wrote a book dealing with the genetic implications of this incident, *The Supplanter Undeceived*, and gave it the subtitle *Jacob's Divine Instruction in Heredity*. What we do know is that Jacob could no more produce this genetic alteration than a French poodle could cause a litter of poodles to be born by running by a pair of German Shepherds at mating time. As unexplainable as the entire operation sounds, we find that God gave Jacob the idea and made it work!

> And it came about at the time when the flock were mating that I lifted up my eyes and saw in a dream, and behold, the male goats which were mating were striped, speckled and mottled. Then the angel of God said to me in the dream, "Jacob," and I said, "Here I am." He said, "Lift up now your eyes and see that all the male goats which are mating are striped, speckled, and mottled; for I have seen all that Laban has been doing to you" (31:10-12).

This is one of the most striking examples in the Bible of God meeting a man where he is.

Jacob's creative energies flowed when he could work an angle with the knowledge that God was actually changing the odds in his favor. God adapted Himself to Jacob in a most creative way in the exact venue that concerned him the most at this juncture of his life. He must have left piles of shavings from whittling branches to place in front of mating animals to perform his part in the speckled goat game that came from the dream God gave him.

This principle that grows out of Jacob's life experience is fundamental to leaders in the process of spiritual formation. Their businesses become an avenue which God uses to meet them uniquely and profoundly.

**Entrepreneurs Still Meet God**

For entrepreneurs a business often becomes their baby, a product of their creativity and passion, their place to stand in life, make their mark, express their identity, and prove to the world that they can compete successfully in the game of life. When I met Angus at a conference for entrepreneurs, our relationship gelled around this core issue. He was a man who was ready to meet God in business. His home and personal agribusiness operation are in Ireland, but he also maintains a residence in the U.S. as a base for his international operations and U.S. projects.

Skills from his doctorate taken in the United Kingdom transferred easily to projects such as an intensive year-long Bible survey process. His laptop work with a Bible software program on long flights easily rival what many seminary students produce.

When we discussed his five-fold business plan for a new year, I was reminded of how his life continues to be intersected by the divine in two of those areas. His international consulting work takes him from the Middle East to Africa, Eastern Europe, South America and the United States. He also attempts to put together large integrated agricultural projects in which production, manufacture of commodities such as ethanol or nutraceuticals, and other functions center around the purchase of large tracts of land. One venture he explored would have doubled dairy production in a small country. When some of these projects are ready to go either way, he is learning to want God's best, however the deal works out.

He completed an extensive biblical study on the Sabbath or day of rest principle because of his business that demands 24/7 availability 365 days per year. Can an agribusiness owner honor God within this kind of schedule? We discussed partnership issues such as involvement with a member of a royal family who was deeply committed to an eastern religion. When he discovered that someone he was considering for a business relationship had gone to a fortune teller for personal and business prognostication, this generated another study on how biblical principles might apply to a relationship with such a person. Angus has a rapport with international agribusiness leaders that missionaries can't access. We worked on his missionary role in these situations, since these relationships warrant talking naturally about basic life issues such as faith, God, and one's spiritual experience. He wants to be prepared to serve God by serving people as a good steward of his unusual career opportunities. Growing and developing in his life journey with God through his multinational agribusiness career is always a part of what we discuss.

Are you finding your career or professional life a place where God is intersecting your life with special opportunities to forge a deeper relationship with Him? God could hardly have met Jacob in any more amazing way than by going into a genetic manipulation business scheme with him. God was giving him an opportunity to learn to live with Him, get to know Him, and to work out his destiny while he pursued his career. He continues to do the same today.

**Family Engineering**

Jacob began to enjoy astonishing success. But building a business was not his only priority. He also did an amazing job of managing his complex and competitive household. His wife Leah longed to be loved and received deeply into his life even though she was not the woman of his dreams (Genesis 29:31-35;30:9-20). Since God let Leah know He cared about her, it's a good thing Jacob considered Leah as well.

When Rachel panicked over not having children, she

gave her maid, Bilhah, to Jacob to have a child in surrogate fashion for her. This was not an uncommon practice in the Middle East. Even though Leah had sons, she also felt constrained to give her maid, Zilpah, to Jacob for more children. She claimed that God rewarded her for this (30:18). During this stressful, competitive time eleven sons and one daughter, Dinah, were born. Jacob built a relationship with each of his sons so that much later his inspired prophecy was given perceptively about each. The tragedy which later happened to Dinah seems to occur in the context of a family where she was nurtured and recognized as a valid person instead of being kept in the family compound like a slave. After she was violated by Shechem and taken into his tent, Simeon and Levi massacred the males in the village (Genesis 34).

Though it was difficult to manage a growing business with the stress and strain at home, Jacob stayed connected with his family. He was building a family which became the nation God was preparing for His plan and purpose in the world. A deeply integrated family unit was formed that became a nation which still survives today.

### So . . . What Is Career?

*What then is a career?* Is it what we do for a living, our *profession*? Is it how we make a name for ourselves, what everybody recognizes? Is it what will be written up in our obituaries in the *Chicago Tribune* or *New York Times?*

When I look at career in the broadest context, I come to one conclusion and this helps free me to look at my own life without all the constraints with which I have judged myself and others. I believe that *a career is comprised of whatever contribution we make in life, however we do it, with God being the final Judge.* This is what I see in the life of Jacob. He approached his entire life from the perspective that *every* aspect of it had its place and value.

## Profession Versus Career

Jacob's outlook on life is confirmed when one looks at the spectacular careers of Bible characters such as Joseph and Esther. Joseph was ripped away from his home by jealous brothers. Eventually, he became the vice-regent of Egypt, one of the most powerful men in the world. He performed with such a high level of excellence that he easily rose above his peers, enjoying spectacular success.

It is the way Joseph viewed his overwhelming professional superiority that surprised me. He saw his professional place in Egypt as a *platform* to support a more essential contribution. He refused any revenge against his brothers because he recognized that his experience in Egypt was not for personal renown, but to prepare a place for his family.

When Esther became Queen of Persia as a Jewess in a foreign land, her Uncle Mordecai helped her realize she was not merely living out a "Queen for a Day" fantasy. She was "Queen for a purpose." Her unexpected rise to royalty gave her a *platform* for her more essential function–preserving her people.

I do not know of any career detailed in the Bible which is treated as an end in itself and not a *platform* for a greater purpose. Neither Joseph nor Esther or Jacob viewed profession as all-encompassing. Their vocations were the means by which they carried out their callings and fulfilled their destinies.

## Finally . . . If You Were at the Podium

Suppose you were to stand and lecture on "Career Concepts for World Class Business Leaders" before a group of internationally acclaimed CEOs in Paris or Johannesburg. What would you wish to emphasize?

Career–what some men and women are willing to die for, what others live for, what others sacrifice their basic relationships for, where some find their greatest opportunity for fulfillment and others heartbreaking failure, where some rise to the top or others end broken and disillusioned, and where a lot of people go quietly about their professions and make a success of their lives.

Is your concept of career big enough? Do you need to make any changes in the way you are living out your career? Any changes for those you are influencing the most?

THE LEADER'S JOURNEY . . .
> **Embracing your calling and career–the contributions you are able to make within the framework of the plan or big picture for your life.**

Questions for Reflection (alone or in a group):

1. How do you describe your career?

2. What do you want to accomplish in it?

3. Do you think the average person has a big enough understanding of what his or her career is? Why?

4. Should we make a distinction between profession or career, or should they be considered as the same thing?

5. What past influences shape the way you look at your career?

6. What would you like to communicate to someone who is troubled, sad or disillusioned about his or her career? What about someone who is intoxicated with his or her success?

**Response**

Thank God for the gift of career and for what you are learning in this critical part of your life.

# CHAPTER 9

# EXILE – LIFE ON A TEST TRACK

*I know how men in exile feed on dreams of hope.*
                                        *Aeschylus*

*Thus I was: by day the heat consumed me and the frost by night, and my sleep fled from my eyes. These twenty years I have been in your house; I served you fourteen years for your two daughters and six years for your flock, and you changed my wages ten times.*
                                        *Genesis 31:40-41*

*His grief he will not forget;*
*but it will not darken his heart, it will teach him wisdom.*
                                        *J. R. R. Tolkien*

# EXILE – LIFE ON A TEST TRACK

Leaders often have exile experiences. Moses was banished to the desert for forty years before he was called back to lead an enslaved nation out of Egypt. Nelson Mandella was locked away twenty-six years but still was able to lead his South African people without directing malice at those responsible for putting him in prison. The great culminating book of the Bible, Revelation, was birthed during the Apostle John's exile on a small rocky island in the Mediterranean.

I don't know if you have gone through an exile experience. At one point in my life it became necessary to take a second job to supplement what my chaplaincy position was not paying. For months I missed nights of sleep because of "Operation Test Track" at a farm implement testing facility. In that fiercely competitive, billion dollar industry, the only way companies can survive is to make sure their machinery holds up under the severe demands of farm work. One night after my shift I looked at the work order on the tractor I was driving; it read, "Run Until Destruction or Test Requirements Fulfilled!" During this time I wondered if this was the work order placed on my life.

My emotions are still strong as I recall those lonely nights fighting sleep piloting a roaring diesel-powered tractor around and around the track. Recently I found a hand-written note penned during one of those long nights: "Tonight, Jo Ann attending Handel's *Messiah*. Wish I could be there." While my stint lasted for a few months, Jacob was headed for a much longer exile–twenty years!

"Run Until Destruction or Test Requirements Fulfilled" around and around a track. That's a good description of an exile experience. You feel like you're not going anywhere, are shoved off on a side track, and have no way back to where you want to be.

Jacob didn't know when he left home that he was headed for twenty years of testing. But that is exactly what his time in Syria with his Uncle Laban proved to be. It was a period of holding up under stress and severe demands so that some things were being burned out of his life while God was building other things into him.

**Seven Laps Around the Track**
After an uneventful journey from Bethel to Haran, Jacob found himself at a well, asking the shepherds who were watering their flocks if they knew his Uncle Laban. Just at that moment Laban's daughter Rachel came to water her flock. Jacob broke down and cried as he introduced himself to his cousin. It was the moment he had been waiting for during his 300-mile journey. Before the end of the day, Jacob was at Laban's home celebrating the family reunion.

Jacob settled in for a month as the "relative from abroad." The thirty days involved more than filling in Laban's family about Isaac, Rebekah and Esau. Jacob fell in love with Rachel, the only woman he would ever deeply love romantically. During his trek east, Jacob probably fantasized about the bride he would acquire when he arrived in Haran. Little did he know that "Miss Universe" was waiting to fall in love with him. There are only two women in the Old Testament to whom all three Hebrew words for physical beauty are applied: one is Esther who became the queen of Persia, even though she was a Jew, and the other is Rachel!

Laban undoubtedly saw what was happening to his daughter and nephew and knew this could be an opportunity to expand his family fortune. After all, a man in love will do crazy things. Perhaps Jacob would agree to work an unusually long period of time to acquire Rachel (according to the custom of the day, one year of service could have earned Rachel's hand in marriage). Laban certainly had to be ecstatic when Jacob agreed to his offer.

Seven years is a long time to work hard with little to no immediate reward. Yet Jacob's love for Rachel was so strong that the years seemed to be only a few days (Genesis 29:20). Finally it was time and Jacob again asked Laban for Rachel. Laban agreed, the wedding feast plans were set, and the big night arrived. And what a night it was. Laban substituted his older daughter Leah for Rachel! Unfortunately, Jacob didn't discover the switch until the morning light!

We will never know how Jacob could be so deceived. Perhaps it was the fact that Leah was brought to him veiled under the cover of darkness. Maybe Jacob had too much to drink. All we know is that he was heartbroken in the morning! Laban's excuse was that the culture demanded that the oldest daughter be married first. He did agree, however, to give Rachel to Jacob *if* he would serve him another seven years.

**Around the Track Another Seven Times!**

Jacob ascended to the upper echelons of great lovers when he accepted Laban's proposal without flinching. He was permitted to marry Rachel after the required period of celebration for his marriage to Leah. Instead, of one year of service for his daughter, Laban got fourteen years (Genesis 29:25-30)!

A honeymoon was not an option. Almost immediately there were problems between the two sisters as they competed for his attention. Jacob was in love with Rachel, but it was Leah who got pregnant and gave birth to a boy (in a culture that especially valued a male child). Their intensity became so unrestrained that each wife gave her servant woman to Jacob so that she did not fall behind in the birth race. During the second seven-year period Jacob served for Rachel, eleven sons and a single daughter were born in quick succession to Leah and Rachel and their two servants, Bilhah and Zilpah. But even though there were many children, there was not much happiness in the family.

There were also problems between Jacob and his father-in-law and brothers-in-law. The conflict escalated to extreme danger when Jacob prospered after Laban gave him some animals as working capital for his own business. Jacob called Rachel and Leah to a field council at his shepherding outpost and spoke to them as his equals, without attempting to dictate their response to the crisis. He reminded them "that I have served your father with all my strength" (31:6). In return, Laban had changed his contract ten times during the last seven years to keep him poor (31:6-7). He cited God's presence (31:5), protection (31:7), and provision (31:9) as the reason for his success, in spite of Laban's best efforts, and concluded with the news of God's command and call to return home (31:13). The response of Rachel and Leah was decisive, reasoned and unequivocal.

Rachel and Leah answered and said to him, "Do we still have any portion or inheritance in our father's house? Are we not reckoned by him as foreigners? For he has sold us, and has also entirely consumed our purchase price. Surely all the wealth which God has taken away from our father belongs to us and our children; now then, do whatever God has said to you" (31:14-16).

They felt disposed of, disinherited, and disconnected from their home. They were ready to leave the only life they had ever known. Their final words concur with Jacob's evaluation that God gave him their father's wealth and that he should do what God was commanding–to return to the land of his birth (31:16).

It took Laban three days to find out that Jacob's household had evaporated out of the land (31:20-22). He was furious and chased Jacob for seven days all the way across the Euphrates to the hill country of Gilead (31:21, 23, 25).

## A Standoff

Laban's clan finally caught up with his fleeing son-in-law. Infuriated, Laban blasted Jacob with words to this effect, "You sneaked off like a thief instead of a son-in-law. You took my daughters as if you had captured them! I would have given you a going-away party with music and everything that goes with it. I retain primary rights over your sons and wives. They are *my* sons and daughters! You didn't even give me the courtesy of being able to say goodbye to them. You've acted like a fool and I could kill you for it!" Indeed, it appears the only reason Laban didn't do harm to Jacob was because of a dream warning him not to do so (Genesis 31:29).

Jacob's accumulated anger of twenty years finally erupted as he endured another of Laban's heavy-handed maneuvers. But this time he knew that Laban couldn't touch him. Anger compressed his words as he spit them out like bullets, and said essentially, "Twenty years I have served with you. Your ewes and female goats got the best of care. You had the healthiest flocks and the highest live birthrate of any shepherd in the area. You can't point to a single ram that was killed for food. No shepherd is required to make up the loss of an animal killed by wild animals, but I did that and even replaced what was stolen! I gave unstinting care to my job with you through the burning days and freezing nights. I have been in your household and employ for twenty years. Fourteen of those were for your daughters and the rest to provide a financial base for my family. During that time, you tried to cheat me by changing my wages ten times." Jacob concludes his outburst with strong testimony about God's intervention on his behalf.

> If the God of my father, the God of Abraham, and the fear of Isaac, had not been for me, surely now you would have sent me away empty-handed. God

has seen my affliction and the toil of my hands, so He rendered judgment last night (31:42).

Laban understood what Jacob was saying. The dream the night before the confrontation warned Laban against bringing harm to Jacob. There was nothing to do except bring as peaceful a resolution to the situation as possible. After a formal peace treaty, Laban said goodbye to his daughters and grandchildren and headed for home.

**"Run Until Destruction or Test Requirements Fulfilled"**
Jacob's words to Laban included three elements. *Daily suffering* was indicated by his capsule statement, "By day the heat consumed me, and the frost by night, and my sleep fled from my eyes" (Genesis 31:40). He twice mentioned *extended adversity*–twenty unrelenting years under his father-in-law (31:38, 41). And then there were the *exorbitant demands* which wore him down (31:38-39). While Jacob maintained the highest standards for shepherding, Laban placed impossible burdens on him that violated any reasonable contractual arrangements of the day.

These things were true. For twenty years Jacob had been locked into a "test track" exile experience. The dividends were not immediate, but they were real. It is breathtaking to consider that Jacob's family–the line of people critical to God's plan for the world–were born during his exile time! His career, which was an indispensable support for his life calling, was launched during this era. Perhaps the Jews' wonderful survival abilities over the centuries can in some way be traced back to Jacob's experience with Laban. That twenty-year period is one of the most productive recorded about any character in the Bible. It is a compelling segment of his epic story.

Are you living in exile, experiencing extended, painful, or hopeless separation from what you want so badly? What could you learn from Jacob? Your career may be a dreary road to nowhere at this time, your marriage a heartbreak special, and with only a few good prospects ahead and many more bad ones. When God has big plans for people, exile experiences are often what He uses to prepare them for future success.

If exile experiences like we endure today were random, without purpose or meaning, a statement like the one in James 1:2 would be foolish: "Consider it all joy, my brethren when you encounter various trials." The process may involve "neck in the yoke and mouth in the dust" (Lamentations 3:27-29), but the end result is a life that is "perfect (not deficient in any vital area) and complete, lacking in nothing" (James 1:3-4).

T.S. Rendall wrote a series of studies on the disciplines of God and entitled them, "God's Discipline of Delay, Detour, Darkness, Deflation, Denial, Defeat, Disturbance, Distress, Dilemma, Destruction, Disappointment, Departure, Disqualification, and Determent." Someone else added Danger, Declining Days, Defamation, Deformity, Desolation, Desperation, Disability, Discontentment, Disdain, Disease, Disillusionment, Domination, and Doubt.

Exile passages in our lives come in all forms, and few of us escape some kind of a *'D'* experience. Yet we can take heart when we read, "All discipline for the moment seems not to be joyful, but sorrowful; yet to those who have been trained by it, afterwards it yields the peaceful fruit of righteousness" (Hebrews 12:11).

Like the tourist who discovered an Indian pipe when he traveled to the Southwest, we often get the wrong message about our own exile circumstances. When he asked for an interpretation of the words inscribed on it, he was expecting a clue to the origins of his valuable artifact. He was surprised by the answer, "Made in Taiwan." It is easy to mistranslate an exile experience. "Messed up" is our initial reaction, but God's intention for us is "Made in exile!"

Have you been able to get beneath the surface of those times when you felt you were on hold to consider a bigger plan or purpose?

THE LEADER'S JOURNEY . . .
**Developing while persevering through difficult seasons and finding God in these times like Jacob did**

Questions for Reflection (alone or in a group):

1. What most resembles an exile experience in your life?

2. How did you react?

3. Do you remember one of your worst "lows"?

4. What did you gain? Did you grow as a person and in your relationship with God?

5. If you have been through an exile experience, is there anything you need to clear up such as remaining anger, fear, bitterness or inability to trust God?

**Response**

Praise (or prayer) for enduring an exile experience and reaping the benefits.

# CHAPTER 10

# PENIEL –
# CRISIS TRANSFORMATION

*We are not capable of union with another on the deepest level*
*until the inner self . . . is sufficiently awakened*
*to confront the inner self of another.*

*Thomas Merton*

*The messengers returned to Jacob, saying, "We came to
your brother Esau, and furthermore he is coming to meet
you, and four hundred men are with him." Then Jacob was
greatly afraid and distressed; and he divided the people who
were with him, and the flocks and the herds and the camels,
into two companies; Then Jacob was left alone, and a man
wrestled with him until daybreak.*

*When he saw that he had not prevailed against him, he
touched the socket of his thigh; so the socket of Jacob's
thigh was dislocated while he wrestled with him. Then he
said, "Let me go, for the dawn is breaking." But he said, "I
will not let you go unless you bless me." So he said to him,
"What is your name?" And he said, "Jacob." He said,
"Your name shall no longer be Jacob, but Israel; for you
have striven with God and with men and have prevailed."*

*So Jacob named the place Peniel, for he said, "I have seen God face to face, yet my life has been preserved."*

*Genesis 32:6-7, 24-28, 30*

*Fire transforms all things it touches into its own nature.*
*The wood does not change the fire into itself.*
*In the same way we are transformed into God.*

*Meister Eckert*

# PENIEL – CRISIS TRANSFORMATION

## Peniel and the Ultima Thule

By engaging Jacob's experience at Peniel, we come in contact with a legendary aspect of human experience. Arctic adventurer Alvah Simon in his brilliantly written book *North to the Night – A Year in the Arctic Ice*, chronicles surviving multiple near-death experiences while he is frozen in for almost a year in his thirty-six-foot sailing sloop, the *Roger Henry*. *Ultima Thule* is a term known to Arctic explorers and adventurers. It refers to a great death-defying episode which changes one's life permanently in some way. It is the *ultimate experience*.

Simon's years-long quest for his *Ultima Thule* led him to a confrontation with a large polar bear. He fell in behind him and called out "Nanook," using his Inuit Eskimo name.

I slowly laid my gun on the ground and stepped toward the bear. That first step, over perhaps only three feet of earth, was actually my final step in a very long journey. I had scoured the earth, skies, and seas to find this. I'd unwittingly passed a hundred moments as ripe with potential as this, but as the mythologist Joseph Campbell said, "We have the adventure for which we are ready." And finally, I was ready. My time alone in the darkness had been but preparation for this. Here, as if it was etched in the delicate tundra grasses, was my line, my edge, my *Ultima Thule*, where a man meets his moment, where the fear passes through him and still he stands, open to every consequence of living and dying.

I took one more step. The bear grunted and rocked forward. I opened my arms, turning my

133

palms to the heavens. The bear stepped toward me. He rose above me, a horrible mountain of fang and claw, crushing power, and lightning speed.

The moment hung in its own eternity. And then the bear spun around and slid away in great strides over the tundra. I stood stunned and faint, my soul indelibly embossed with the bear's message: "Here, I give you back life. It has been washed pure by your fear. Enjoy it deeply, learn from it daily, and use it wisely, for there is a purpose larger than yourself."

Alvah Simon's lesser experience in surviving his terrifying run-in with the bear points to Jacob's greater one. When he emerged from his Peniel experience, he said, "I have seen God face to face, yet my life has been preserved" (Genesis 32:30). Surviving the infinite in an *Ultima Thule* experience, when one faces death on one hand and God on the other and there is no place else to go, is what this chapter is about.

## Leaders in Crisis!

Most of us find our Peniel-type experience forced on us, and it is often unexpected. When Philip said he wanted to talk over lunch about challenges he was facing, I assumed it was about routine issues. It wasn't! One of the 150 drivers in his freight firm rear-ended a van in a highway construction site, killing a woman and small child. A few days later, another of his drivers, attempting to be a Good Samaritan, pulled behind a disabled truck in order to offer assistance. Though his flashers were on, another truck slammed into Philip's truck and killed the driver in the stalled vehicle.

Philip had a million-dollar insurance policy in place for such a catastrophe, but it was proving to be insufficient, and now Philip was talking with bankruptcy attorneys. The jobs of his 200 employees were at stake.

Michael, a CFO, retired in his forties with a platinum parachute when his billion-dollar firm was sold, called me with an urgent prayer request. His active, athletic wife, who ran marathons and climbed mountains, had just been diagnosed with cancer. The cells had metastasized in the lymph nodes.

Horrendous crises can barge into our lives without notice. They level the playing field of humanity whether we are at the bottom or top or in between. They create circumstances that change our lives forever.

Jacob knew about living with crises. They were the story of his life. Now, on the eve of meeting Esau after twenty years, the big confrontation will become being *alone with the Alone* during the severest crisis he had ever faced (George Maloney). The venue becomes Peniel, Hebrew for *the face of* God. We pay a high price for an *Ultima Thule* or Peniel experience, and we must be prepared or it can become a disaster. Jacob was ready for this confrontation with the Alone because of his own twenty-year preparation and also because he had no choice!

### No Contest!

As Jacob approached his homeland, he sent messengers to make contact with Esau (Genesis 32:3). The report came back that Esau was returning with a band of 400 men. It was like 400 green berets meeting a squad of summer reserves on a picnic with their families. It was *nolo contendere*–no contest! Jacob's animals, servants and family members were completely vulnerable.

Apparently, Jacob forgot a huge sign from God that he would not be harmed. Just before he learned that Esau and 400 men were heading his way, the angels of God met Jacob. He recognized them ("This is God's host") because he had seen angels at Bethel years earlier (28:12). Just as at Bethel, he immediately consecrated the place with a name,

*Mahanaim*, a Hebrew term meaning "two camps" in reference to his own entourage and the group of angels or the angels appearing in two divisions. But the significance of God's angels seemed lost on Jacob. He failed to realize that God's army of angels could make Esau's 400 men no more significant than flies buzzing around harmlessly.

After he heard the news of Esau's entourage, "Jacob was greatly afraid and distressed" (32:7). He prayed a desperate plea, "O God of my father Abraham and God of my father Isaac." Jacob prayed with an inherited reality of God from his father and grandfather. "Deliver me, I pray, from the hand of my brother, from the hand of Esau; for I fear him, lest he come and attack me, the mothers with the children." Sometimes it is difficult for a man to choke out his confession of fear for himself and his family.

Before Jacob asked God to remember that He was the One who told Jacob to return home, he made a confession: "I am unworthy of all the lovingkindness and of all the faithfulness which You have shown to Your servant; for with my staff only I crossed this Jordan, and now I have become two companies" (Genesis 32:10). If you were in the worst crisis you ever faced, would you tell God first that you didn't deserve His intervention? In the face of death, Jacob gives evidence that he has grown significantly since Bethel when he wanted God to agree to contract stipulations before he would agree to be His servant.

Jacob begged God for mercy and kindness. He was on solid ground because God had promised to bless Jacob with descendents who would be as numerous as the sands on the seashore. Jacob's fate and that of every member of his family, along with his ambitions, plans and possessions were all out of his hands. *In his prayer he transferred them to God.*

Jacob prayed as if his life and the lives of his family depended on God. But he was still a cunning strategist who came up with a plan to appease Esau. And so, he offered his brother a generous gift . . . or a bribe (it didn't matter to Jacob as long as Esau was happy), 550 head of livestock–enough to make a person instantly wealthy. He hoped Esau would be impressed by the evidence of Jacob's success.

**Wrestle Mania**
A blacksmith heats a piece of metal until it is red hot and then strikes an insignificant blow with a small hammer. This place marks the spot where the heavy sledge will smash the metal to mold it to its final shape. God had brought Jacob to Bethel and marked his life for years of formation. He had been in the fire for twenty years and said as much (Genesis 31:40-41)! Now he was on the anvil to receive the "molding blow" in which he would be permanently injured, limping away with a new name and ultimately a new identity.

His time *alone with the Alone* along the banks of the Jabbok River provided the context which Brother Roger of Taize describes, "In every one lies a zone of solitude that no human intimacy can fill; and there God encounters us." He couldn't have imagined how he was to be prepared for his meeting with Esau.

After sending his wives and children across the Jabbok River, Jacob was alone in his camp, suspended between the only two worlds he knew. The door to Laban's house was shut forever. The only other place for Jacob was the land to which he had been commanded to return. Yet Esau stood in the way. As he weighed his predicament, something froze Jacob's attention, a dim shadow of a figure. Was it Esau the aggressor? The thought must have made him sick. He might not even live to the next day! He reacted with the pent-up fury, fear or frenzy that can make one man a temporary match for several. There was nothing left to do but attack. And attack is what Jacob did, fighting all night with the assailant.

As the wrestling match continued through the night, a

stark reality forced its way into Jacob's traumatized senses: "It's not Esau and it's not one of his men. I don't know who it is, but he is not my enemy." Imperceptibly, he began to understand that his opponent had come primarily as a solution and secondarily as a wrestler. He realized he did not have to fight his unknown partner, but also knew he would not give up the fight without some answers.

As the morning light began to dawn, the contestant touched Jacob's hip joint and crippled him for life. Jacob's injury became so sacred to successive generations of Jews that they refused to eat the meat from this part of an animal (Genesis 32:32).

Now Jacob was exhausted and injured. He could no longer stand or walk without a limp, but he could still cling (32:26). When his opponent demanded, "Let me go, for the dawn is breaking," Jacob's response was simple and desperate, "I will not let You go unless You bless me" (32:26). Here was a man of God contending for the blessing of God. And Jacob's desperate demand for "blessing" was granted! (32:29)

**What's in a Name?**

The all-important blessing was preceded by an unexpected question, "What is your name?" And he said, "Jacob" (32:27). Jacob's life was pictured in his name. "I am a heel grabber!" But things were about to change. The Wrestler said, "Your name shall no longer be Jacob, but Israel. You have become a prince, a prevailer, one who has power with God and with men."

At this startling announcement, Jacob asked, "Please tell me Your name," only to be asked another question, "Why do you ask My name?"

The One who names must be greater than the one who is named. Did the mystery Wrestler have sufficient authority to change Jacob's name and identity? Of course! Jacob named the place Peniel, "Face of God," and received the blessing of the divine Wrestler.

Some people find the question, "What is your name?" terrifying because it seeks an identity. Too often the answer is, "I could never tell you who I am. I don't know who I am, or I can't even admit who I am to myself. I look successful, but I'm messed up. I would trade my big home to stop what I continue doing but keep hidden from everybody. I'll probably never get straightened out."

The forced solitude and struggle at Peniel can be a model for us. Robert Mulholland captures it well.

This is what solitude is: in the silence of releasing control of our relationship with God to God, coming face to face with the kind of person we are in the depths of our being; seeing the depths of our grasping manipulative, self-indulgent behavior; facing the brokenness, the darkness, the uncleanness that is within; acknowledging our bondages, our false securities, our posturing facades; and naming ourselves to God as this kind of person . . . In silence we let go our manipulative control. In solitude we face up to what we are in the depths of our being. Prayer then becomes the offering of who we are to God: the giving of that broken, unclean, grasping, manipulative self to God for the work of God's grace in our lives (p. 140).

At Peniel we face ourselves. We hear our name. We confess who we are, no matter how bad it looks and feels. The awesome reality is that God enters into our broken lives to identify what He sees us to be (2 Corinthians 5:17). His pronouncement assures the result. When He says, "It is ISRAEL, Prince with God" (instead of Jacob, the heel grabber), then ISRAEL it really is!

**Wrestling Lessons**

Jacob contended with the Lord to get something he didn't have to become, something he could never be on his own . . . a prince with God! The Old Testament prophet Hosea summarizes Jacob's life from the prenatal to Peniel in this fashion: "In the womb he took his brother by the heel, and in his maturity he contended with God. Yes, he wrestled with the angel and prevailed; he wept and sought His favor" (12:3-4).

There was a mysterious, unformed grabbing in Jacob's life which began with cleverness and deceit, but culminated at Peniel where he contended with God and prevailed. Four verbs are used in this Hosea passage, "wrestled, prevailed, wept, and sought."

What is the point? Jacob, Prince with God, is held up as a model to those who bear his name. In the previous two verses, the prophet notes that their pursuits are directed to every other place but God, resulting in disaster (Hosea 12:1-2). Now, they are to be like Jacob, *wrestling* with God. They should *weep* while they hang on to Him at midnight when death may come the next day. Hosea tells the people to *seek* Him even though they are injured and brokenhearted. Finally, they will *prevail* with God and He will bless them with what He has been waiting and wanting to give.

**Peniel and the Torture Track Principle**

From Jacob's time until now, God's people have spent time in circumstances that could be likened to a "torture track" while select chapters of their lives are being written.

I spent one shift on the torture track. While I was test-driving tractors, the order finally came, "You're on the torture track tonight!" The tractor I was assigned had more than 4,000 pounds of extra weight attached to the front axle (equivalent to two compact cars) and had to be driven over large ridges with speed bumps for the entire shift. I jammed my feet across the windshield crossbar to prevent back injury and was thrown into the ceiling. Nothing helped. Months of testing were compressed into hours on the torture track to get a production model tractor for use around the world. Soon after my shift on the torture track, it began to be called the "Nebraska Strip." Stoic men were excited. Tests which destroyed equipment and punished the people who drove them were finished! One of our tractors was being shipped to Nebraska to become a production model for use around the world.

That's what happened to Jacob at Peniel–he became a production model! He spent twenty years on the *test track* with Uncle Laban and endured a stint on the *torture track* at Peniel. At sunrise the next day he limped out with his model designation, *Prince with God*. So that's what God is doing at our Peniels as well–making us production models to stand the test of time and *beyond*! Just as Kenneth Caraway once wrote, "There is no box . . . but that the sides can be flattened out and the top blown off to make a dance floor on which to celebrate."

Peniel is not primarily a package but a principle. Jacob's *Ultima Thule* encounter at Peniel was limited to a few square yards along a small river flowing from the eastern frontier in Gilead to the Jordan. Time limitations made it an experience of twelve hours or less (Genesis 32:22, 24).

Your Peniel may extend halfway around the world through burning days and anguished months. The predetermined end is the same. *In the darkness of a major life crisis, a permanent forward step is taken in God's foundational plan for your life.* He uses an arena of focused interests, drives, or motivations to lead you to wrestle from Him the blessing of a lifetime. In some great suffocating experience, what is so twisted into the fabric of a life structure without any possibility of being changed *can be changed!* This is the Peniel Principle!

Peniel becomes an opportunity to discover a renowned part of the plan God has for your life, just as Jacob did when he began the night terrified of Esau and left in triumph as Israel, Prince with God. He prevailed in an experience he would have avoided at all costs before it happened. We may be called to do the same!

THE LEADER'S JOURNEY . . .
> **Meeting God when He is your last resort.
> Finding God while facing the loss of every-
> thing else and gaining a life that won't be
> the same and can't be as small as before.**

Questions for Reflection (alone or in a group):

1. What was most significant to you from this Peniel chapter of Jacob's life?

2. Do any of your experiences parallel what happened to
   Jacob at Peniel?

3. How would you explain what happened to Jacob and its
   application to people today?

4. Have you seen anyone go through a Peniel type
   episode? How might the career of a leader be changed
   significantly by an intense ordeal like Peniel?

**Response**

Prayer/praise for the manner in which God meets (has met)
you in the dark and desperate times to bring change or transformation.

# CHAPTER 11

# SURVIVING MIDLIFE AND FINISHING WELL

*For the great majority of men . . .*
*Midlife Transition is a time of moderate or severe crisis . . . .*
*They cannot go on as before,*
*but need time to choose a new path or modify the old one.*
*Daniel J. Levinson*

*Jacob journeyed to Succoth, and built for himself a house and made booths for his livestock; therefore the place is named Succoth.*

*Now Jacob came safely to the city of Shechem, which is in the land of Canaan, when he came from Paddan-aram, and camped before the city.*

*He bought the piece of land where he had pitched his tent from the hand of the sons of Hamor, Shechem's father, for one hundred pieces of money.*

*Then he erected there an altar and called it El-Elohe-Israel.*

*Genesis 33:17-20*

*The man journeying to his own country
must not mistake the inn for his home.*

*Augustine*

# SURVIVING MIDLIFE AND FINISHING WELL

## Men at Midstream

Men get beaten up in life. If they succeed in business, they are still beaten up. They want rest. They want respite. They want shelter. They want relief from stress.

Men who have made it by the time they reach their fifties often want to "cash out," perhaps to sell a business and do something else. Some build a cabin away from it all, savoring the idea of retreating and finding rest. They retreat to this second home where they can run the business for a couple of months a year.

Jack set up an appointment to see me just after he finished a meeting with potential buyers who represented a conglomerate. He pulled out his quarterly report indicating a record month. I first met him when his monthly gross was around $300,000. New estimates predict that his business will be worth $75,000,000 in two to three years.

He kicked off his shoes and walked over to sit down. It wasn't the first time he spoke of being tired. "I came into this business when I was sixteen, and in seven years I will have done the equivalent of two military careers."

As I reflected with him, I said, "Jack, you have two questions you need to consider. You shouldn't make a decision because you are tired and feel beaten up. You need to answer two questions before you think seriously about selling, to determine the 'why and what.' *Why are you living and **what** are you supposed to do with your life?*"

## Jacob after Peniel

Jacob was like many men today–a survivor, successful after beating the odds, tired and vaguely discouraged even though others may envy them. "There comes a time when a man must think about himself," we say.

It was a minor miracle that Jacob made it to Succoth and Shechem. Some translators say he came to Shalem in Shechem and others that he arrived in Shechem "safe and sound." It was a celebration just to be there!

Esau could have killed him before he left home. His twenty years with Uncle Laban were filled with deprivation and danger. When he finally fled and Laban caught up with him, Jacob released his pent-up anger (Genesis 31:36-41), remembering the fourteen years of servitude, ten wage changes in the final six years, periods of separation from his family, unfair working conditions in which he had to replace animals that were killed or lost when the code of the day called for the owner to do so, freezing at night in the harsh desert and baking during the day in the searing heat. And his reward? Laban's sons (his cousins) turned against him perhaps to murder him if he didn't run first.

Life certainly had not been easy for Jacob. His success had come at a high price. Even when he returned home he faced the prospect of retaliation from Esau. His anxiety subsided as Esau and his 400 men disappeared toward their home base at Seir in Edom to the south. The reconciliation was genuine, but the terrible memories persisted–running for his life from his home as a young man and facing the threat of having his own life and everyone else dear to him destroyed by Esau when he returned home.

Jacob was tired and wounded. How many men today can hardly fight back tears when they get into selected segments of their own memory disks? What do they want? Some want to be sheltered for a while, to escape the unrelenting stress of their lives. After all, there is a limit to how long a person can survive on the front line–even if he doesn't get shot. "Just a little peace for a while. Is that too much to ask?"

Jacob desperately longed for relief. He wanted to live as a free man in his native country. As he headed west, travel-ing away from Esau, he made two stops. First, Jacob journeyed to Succoth, and "built for himself a house, and made booths for his livestock. Therefore the place is named Succoth" (33:17). Jacob didn't build houses like ours. He pitched tents and made shelters for himself, his family and livestock with the hope of getting out of the storm, off the front line and on the lee side of the harsh winds that had blown against him for the last twenty years. It's rather like what you see when you travel to Florida in the wintertime. One Sunday, I visited a church in Fort Myers. The parking lot was filled with SUVs and luxury cars. I met a retired Sears executive who had lived an hour from us before he moved. "Fort Myers is really a bustling areas with its own congestion," I said. "What is driving this economy?" His response was simple and direct. "People retire and bring their money down here. You ought to see some of the homes. They cost two to three million."

Men and women finish their frontline duty. Whether it's Fort Myers, Scottsdale, Aspen or West Palm Beach–it's a Succoth, a place of shelter, pleasure and rest. How long do these men and women stay in Florida? Some until they die! But they are further along in their lives than Jacob was when he came to Succoth.

How long did Jacob stay in Succoth? Some scholars say Jacob wasn't in Succoth for even a year and others say several years–long enough for Dinah to get in the trouble she found in Shechem. But it's not the length of time Jacob spent in Succoth that is important; it's the principle of his Succoth experience. He stayed until he felt restored enough to move on. His family could be settled for a while and his herds fed and strengthened for the next leg of the trip. The rest of his life did not hold this peaceful "Florida lifestyle." Succoth and Shalem in Shechem were brief stops ending in another severe crisis, which could have cost Jacob his life and his entire family as well (34:30).

## In the Land of Shechem

Jacob and his family arrived safely in Canaan and came to Shechem across the Jordan just west of Succoth. His grandfather, Abraham, came here on the way from Ur and built one of his frequent altars (Genesis 12:6-7).

Now Jacob came safely to the city of Shechem, which is in the land of Canaan, when he came from Paddan-aram, and camped before the city. He bought the piece of land where he had pitched his tent from the hand of the sons of Hamor, Shechem's father, for one hundred pieces of money. Then he erected there an altar and called it El-Elohe-Israel. (33:18-20).

Jacob was back, this time with the family he could only dream about when he ran from the land with instructions to marry someone in his Uncle Laban's family. It is not clear whether he came to a village, Shalem, near the city of Shechem or just returned safely. Shalem means peace, and Jacob was finding shelter and peace after twenty years of stressful living.

It is the same concern Jack and I considered: "What do these stops in Succoth and Shalem have to do with the **why** and **what** of Jacob's life?" When he settled his camp near the town gate and purchased property, was it for an extended stay? Or, like King David, did he purchase a plot of ground to have a sacred spot to build his first altar after arriving to give God glory for his safe return?

Whatever the reason, this period of time was only a parenthesis to catch his breath and find strength. **Why** was he living? Certainly not to buy a little piece of land. God promised the whole of it to him! It is already his in trust.

**What** was his mission? What was he supposed to do with his life at this stage? It wasn't to sit around with the local Canaanite sheiks at the city gate.

Whenever we go to the Greek fishing village of Tarpon Springs on the Gulf side of Florida, I walk along Athens Street to a coffee shop where the local Greeks congregate for a dollar cup of Greek coffee. The men are always sitting around talking and playing cards, with one or two sitting alone watching the TV above the door. Not unlike these men, the men of Shechem were sitting around talking and passing time 4,000 years ago. This kind of life was not why God called Jacob. He was called to the journey, to live out the purpose and mission assigned to him at Bethel.

While we were talking, Jack went back to his desk. He opened his calendar and began to scratch a line through every week in June. "What are you doing, Jack?" "I am taking a sabbatical," he replied. "I've never had one." He looked around his office and said quietly, "Everything in this office is charged with memories of stress for me."

We talked on a few minutes and he opened up his calendar again and scratched some more. A little worried about him I asked, "What are you doing now?" "I'm taking another week," he answered. In another few minutes, he said in a reflective manner, "Maybe I'm thinking about selling my business just to get a sabbatical!" Profound!

Maybe Jacob was avoiding the **why** and **what** of his life a little while just to take a sabbatical from the unrelenting stress of his life of pilgrimage to which he was called.

Jacob was in the same place as today's tired men in their forties and fifties. Maybe it's time for them to stop and build an El-Elohe-Israel altar. Jacob came to this Shechem altar with all his heart. God was the God of who he was and who he hoped to be. The issue was staying the course and fulfilling the why and what of his life. Sabbatical . . . Succoth . . . Shechem . . . Shalem . . . time to move on. Anything short of living out the **why** and **what** of our lives is just that–falling short!

**Good Medicine**

While working on this chapter, I looked through a book I had purchased at a mentoring conference and noted a slip of paper with scrawled notes. Two words were circled which I had written, **why** and **what**. I am at a stage of life when I am often tired–tired in the struggle to take another mountain for which I have asked God, tired as I attempt to balance my life which is pulled in various directions. I want the *why* and the *what* of my life to be kept at the forefront, even when I push back for a while.

Like Jacob, so many men today come to a place in their lives when they feel an overwhelming desire for dropping back, chilling out, powering down, having a midlife crisis, resting and recreating, or "coming away for a while."

Outstanding Christian leaders sometimes start fast out of the chute and die in the backstretch. Why don't you settle now on **why** you are living and **what** you are supposed to be doing? Then, be sure it is a passion and not a casual pastime. Like Jacob, you will be able to move on in your journey instead of stalling indefinitely.

THE LEADER'S JOURNEY . . .

**Surviving midlife–staying on track by pursuing the *why* and *what* of your life even though you want an easier way**

Questions for Reflections (alone or in a group):

1.  Think about a period in your life when you felt you couldn't go on without getting away for a while to find rest, respite or restoration. Can you describe this experience?

2.  What did you do about it? What were the results?

3.  If you are having trouble coping, are stressed out or feel you can't go on, how do you maneuver through these times?

4.  How do you keep the **why** and **what** of your life in focus?

5.  What action step should you take as a result of studying this chapter in Jacob's life?

**Response**

Prayer for perseverance to live well with God through the various stages of life (particularly midlife) and cross the finish line as a winner.

# CHAPTER 12

# JOURNEYING TOWARD ARRIVING – BACK TO BETHEL

＋══＋

*The spiritual life cannot be made suburban. It is always frontier.*

*Howard Macey*

*Jacob said, "O God of my father Abraham and God of my father Isaac, O LORD.*
*I am unworthy of all the lovingkindness and of all the faithfulness which You have shown to Your servant; for with my staff only I crossed this Jordan, and now I have become two companies."*

*Genesis 32:9-10*

*In one sense we are always traveling, and*
*traveling as if we did not know where we are going.*
*In another sense we have already arrived.*
*We cannot arrive at the perfect possession*
*of God in this life,*
*and that is why we are traveling and in darkness.*
*But we already possess Him by grace,*

*and therefore, in that sense,*
*we have arrived and are dwelling in the light.*
*But oh! How far have I to go to find You*
*in Whom I have already arrived.*

*Thomas Merton*

## JOURNEYING TOWARD ARRIVING –
## BACK TO BETHEL

Leaders who are journeying with God know that success depends on their IQ–not their *Intelligence Quotient*, but their *INTEGRATION Quotient*. Those who have a high level of Integration Quotient integrate what they believe into their lives in such a way that it makes a significant difference in how they react under pressure, make tough decisions which have long-term consequences, and respond to others who are not always pleasant.

The *Integration Quotient* aspect of your life is determinative. Integrating the realities of God's call and presence deeply into the fabric of your daily decisions and leadership determines spiritual success or failure. Your *Integration Quotient* is measured not only daily but over the long haul. You have probably been shamed over something you did, troubled over a terrible attitude, or repulsed when a perverted thought assaulted you, and may have reacted by saying, "I really haven't changed that much." There are disappointing aspects and incidents in every life. However, *Integration Quotient* is not measured by a few of our experiences, be they good or bad, but rather, over the course of time.

Even when you are disappointed with yourself, it is possible to see how deeply and fundamentally you have changed. It's like climbing a mountain when every step is difficult and when there are times of regression. Yet when you look back, the panorama below is strikingly beautiful. You are moving toward the summit even though your exhausted progress isn't always exhilarating. You are part of a pilgrim people, journeying toward arriving even though your path is rough and ragged.

Three of the men whose lives we have intersected in previous chapters demonstrate a developed *Integration Quotient*. Clayton worked closely with a Christian developer to build a new plant with twice the square footage for his manufacturing company. Some time after the facility was built, his friend informed Clayton that he would gain a million dollars if he bought the building. His cash flow made the purchase possible, but he refused the offer. When I asked him why, he answered, "At this time, I don't think the Lord wants a million dollars from me. I think He wants me." Some might question Clayton's stewardship, but few can doubt his serious attempt to journey with God as an internationally respected business leader.

We talked with Thomas when he was profoundly influenced by the idea of "staying in the box," finding completeness and the highest levels of real success in the defined parameters of his life. In his early forties, he was surprised at the high profile his life had assumed as a friend and influencer of political leaders and as a highly respected leader among restaurateurs.

After a couple of years in the spotlight, he spent several weeks taking a thorough personal inventory. He wanted to be certain of the areas in which he was to focus his energies and what the elements of his life should be. The day-to-day operations of his restaurant (which served about 10,000 meals per week) could be left to his managers. Should he stay close to his restaurant or move into other opportunities? It became plain to Thomas that he needed to be in touch with the people the restaurant served. After this, I saw him on the floor much more frequently. He also determined that his family needed him to be available in presence, not just emotionally. His life evaluation caused him to curtail his involvement in such areas as serving on boards. But he carefully retained other responsibilities such as developing a radio program devoted to a wide range of topics for Greek families in metro Chicago.

Another example of this *Integration Quotient* is Conner. Just after a test revealed stomach cancer, I met him for lunch and noted his deep and sincere peace of mind. With a laugh he shared a telephone conversation that his wife overheard, "If my wife is unfortunate enough that I survive . . ." He was vintage Conner with his normal dry humor. I knew what was motivating him. He is an unusual person in that he brings his melancholic, deeply artistic personality to the numbers-bound world of finance. A heart to know God motivates him as he is frequently being pulled in different directions. In his life-threatening situation, the light of faith in the core of his being was his most dominant reaction.

As we consider the experiences of Jacob when he returned to his homeland, we will discover indicators of a healthy *Integration Quotient.*

**Journeying Toward Arriving**

Jacob was literally *journeying toward arriving* at his place of destiny, his physical journey pointing toward the emotional and spiritual journey that applies to us all. Jacob was seriously engaged in the process of becoming who God made him to be, while fulfilling his immediate roles in life. In the New Testament the Apostle Paul summarized the process in terms of *being* God's masterpiece and *doing* special tasks according to His plan (Ephesians 2:10).

Compelling evidence is present in Jacob's life after his exile in Syria that he was integrating who he *was* and what he *did* into the structure of his life. We see six indicators that he was maturing in his relationship with God, signposts that say, "You are traveling in the right direction; you are journeying toward arriving!"

**Peniel – Transparency**

Jacob's nighttime confrontation with God at Peniel (chapter 10) was a pivotal point in his life. Compared to how he deceived his father to get Esau's blessing, Jacob had become remarkably *transparent.* When he misled his father, his success depended on how well he disguised his identity. Now he was forced to shed his disguise.

We see how he interacted with God. His cry, "O God," tells us that he is now too desperate to be anything more that he is, naked and vulnerable. His statement that he is not worthy of the least of the Lord's mercies confirms this. It is as if he is saying, "You are welcome to see me through and through for who and what I am." He reminds God of His promises (Genesis 32:10, 12) after admitting he doesn't deserve what God promised to do.

Transparency is an exceptional quality that few people possess. Being uncomfortable with oneself, with others, and with God is common. John Powell's book *Why Am I Afraid to Tell You Who I Am?* addresses our inability to be transparent to let people see us as we are. The transparent person is not claiming to be perfect, but is saying you are free to look into his life. The shades are not drawn.

For a spiritual person the issue is not hiding from God but rather giving God full access into his life so that whatever darkness remains may become light. Paul the Apostle took this one step further when he said, "But by the grace of God I am what I am" (1 Corinthians 15:10). Perhaps we can say, "Where I am with all my limitations is by God's grace, and where I might be special or significant is by grace too. Have a look if you wish!" Are you becoming more free to let God and other people see you as you are? Jacob was now that kind of person, and his transparency is the first indicator of a healthy *Integration Quotient*.

### Peniel – Transformation

In the pinnacle experience at Peniel, Jacob's transparency led to *transformation*. Jacob got what sincere leaders long for–a fundamental change that would alter the remainder of his life. The next morning, he came limping into his camp looking not much different than he always did. (Only Moses had a strange and brilliant light about him after he met with God.) The rest of us still halt along as well, much like we always have, even though we are experiencing life-altering metamorphosis.

## El-Elohe-Israel – God of My Deepest Being

After his Peniel experience and just after leaving Esau, Jacob built an altar that he called *El-Elohe-Israel*. The commonly accepted meaning of this title is *God, the God of Israel*. Certainly Jacob was acknowledging that God was his Elohim, the Strong One who delivered him from everything he experienced in his twenty-year exile. But I believe there is more to the designation.

Jacob was also expressing his growing intimacy with God. He was naming his delivering Lord as the God of all that he was or ever could be. He was expressing the profound reality that God is bigger than any experience or blessing He gives us. God stands above and beyond His benefits, even deliverance from death. These things led Jacob beyond the wonder of what God *does* to God Himself. He would never outgrow the God who is all in all.

I remember a time when, in a desperate situation, I prayed earnestly a somewhat strange prayer, "Lord, if you answer my prayer, I promise not to love You any more than I do now!" Why did I pray this prayer? Once we build an El-Elohe-_____(my name or yours), we understand that God is always greater or more wonderful than the abundant array of His favors. We see beyond the scope of His blessings to God as paramount and infinite for us personally.

Have you had your own El-Elohe- _____ (your name) experience? Are you in contact at the deep levels of your being with who you are, what is driving you, or even what you long for but don't have words to describe? Have you found God or at least invited Him into this level of your experience so that He stands over everything that pertains to you?

## Back to Bethel – Coming Clean

After Jacob's El-Elohe-Israel experience, he received marching orders to his next assignment. "Arise, go up to Bethel and live there, and make an altar there to God, who appeared to you when you fled from your brother Esau" (Genesis 35:1). Remember that Jacob's life fell within geographical parameters. It was time to go *back to Bethel* to see how his relationship with God had developed.

The command was symbolic, as if God was saying, "Jacob, go back to where it all began with us." Does the God of the universe feel a transcendent sentimentality like a husband who wants to return with his wife of twenty years to the place they were engaged? In Ezekiel 16 we discover that the answer is a resounding "Yes," because God pictures His relationship with Israel in the intimate terms of a man who woos a woman.

Jacob knew Bethel as a sacred place and thus responded quickly with a preparatory step. He and his family could not be ready for Bethel until they dealt with a lingering issue.

So Jacob said to his household and to all who were with him, "Put away the foreign gods which are among you, and purify yourselves and change your garments; and let us arise and go up to Bethel, and I will make an altar there to God, who answered me in the day of my distress and has been with me wherever I have gone" (Genesis 35:2-3).

It was only at this juncture that he demanded that family idols be put away, and his entire household joined with him in purifying themselves in preparation for a Bethel recommitment. Leah and Rachel had lived in a pagan environment all their lives, but by now they had seen Jacob's faith in action, participated in God's intervention at Peniel, and observed how God made their husband a wealthy man. Having children with Jacob also brought about their own interaction with God. Now it was time to have a religious house cleaning. Removing the pagan idols before they all joined with him to share in his Bethel confirmation was a watershed experience.

Authentic leaders have an opportunity to inspire an infectious sanctity when it is modeled out of their inner core. The pace of life today and the flood of sensory invasions we face daily work against being able to live with God in a special place for very long. In the Life Serve program, we encourage periodic retreats and work on discovering how to be in the presence of God.

Have distractions slowly cluttered your life with off-center practices, leaving your home in a haze of blurred values? Perhaps the habit of watching TV has long ago replaced family prayer time. Are there videos that need discarding? Are you glancing at pornography on the Internet or avoiding spiritual disciplines that are a must for your journey with God? An exorbitant number of possessions easily become idols because they suffocate spirituality and reduce life to managing stuff. Is the same word coming to you or your family, "Put away . . ."?

You need to come clean if you are to pursue God. Are there objects or behaviors that need to be removed from your life or your household? Being uncompromisingly honest, giving others the freedom to ask the hard questions, and letting the implications of returning to your spiritual roots and commitments, like Jacob and his household did, is part of this ongoing process.

## El-Bethel – God of My Greatest Experiences

For Jacob, the command to return to Bethel was a profound invitation. Remember that the dimensions of his entire life were given at Bethel. God became his ultimate *I AM* when He stood above the ladder and spoke to Jacob. Thomas Merton wrote words which ring true for both of Jacob's Bethel experiences: "We already possess Him by grace, and therefore, in that sense, we have arrived and are dwelling in light. But oh! How far have I to go to find You in whom I have already arrived."

Jacob had traveled a long way down the road toward arriving, since his first trip to Bethel. God was very present when Jacob built his *El-Bethel* altar. He appeared to Jacob, blessed him and said:

> "Your name is Jacob; you shall no longer be called Jacob, but Israel shall be your name." Then He called him Israel. God also said to him, "I am God Almighty; be fruitful and multiply; a nation and a company of nations shall come from you, and kings shall come forth from you. The land that I gave to Abraham and Isaac, I will give to you, and I will give the land to your descendants after you" (Genesis 35:10-12).

God never runs out of graces, and one barometer of our relationship with Him is the ability to see not only the repetition but the progression of how He enriches our lives.

Jacob was again named *Israel*, Prince with God. Again, God confirmed Jacob as the one chosen to continue the covenant to Abraham. Such repeated and amplified experiences drive the knowledge of God and His call on our lives even deeper into the inner core of who we are and how we live in this world.

Note the personal overtone as this incident concludes (35:13-15). When Jacob left this place where God spoke with him, it was like a parting of dear friends in which the very place where they met and communicated was memorialized. Think about your own experience. Do you have those times and places in your memory when God's presence and interaction with you seemed very real? Could you describe one of these occurrences, if you have been walking with God for some time?

Jacob responded in a mature manner by anointing his altar with oil a second time. God reminded Jacob earlier that when he ran from Laban (31:13), Jacob anointed a pillar with oil and made a vow to Him. The oil and the altar were symbolic–God had no need of them. God has no need of what we give to Him either. But what we give represents a relationship, a covenant or a commitment. God, who needs nothing, accepts it because He receives us. God has no great need of $50 million from the sale of your business, but He does want you, and will graciously use the funds received in a divine/human partnership.

Returning to Bethel expressed a relationship with God that had grown deeper, more fully committed and centered. Jacob's name for his second Bethel altar reflected this reality. It is *El-Bethel*, which means "the God of Bethel." Returning to Bethel was a reference point for how Jacob's life had changed since he first came to Bethel. Jacob's return to Bethel indicated he was staying centered and growing deeper.

The harsh realities of life didn't stop during this special time for Jacob and his family. Deborah, Rebekah's nurse, died about the time Jacob built his *El-Bethel* altar (35:8). When Isaac died, Jacob and Esau united for the last time to bury him. The crushing blow was when Rachel, the love of Jacob's life, died giving birth to Benjamin. The final hammer blow was delivered by Reuben, Jacob's firstborn, when he violated Bilhah who had given birth to two of his brothers.

A centered life with God does not mean our circumstances will always be pleasant. But Jacob lived in such a way that he was prepared for his continued climb to the summit. In the same way, our greatest happenings with God are not to be fossilized. When we move to an *El-Bethel* stage, we understand that God exceeds the most spectacular of the experiences that come our way. If we do not internalize this reality, challenging situations will cause us to question whether our experience of God is real. Even good things such as our religious practices can stagnate without an *El-Bethel* experience. If you have an *El-Bethel* place in your soul, it is another indication that you are journeying toward arriving at a strong *Integration Quotient*.

### Journeying Toward Arriving – All the Way!

Years later when a famine decimated Canaan, Jacob began the final leg of his journey by moving to Egypt. As he began the trip, God made contact again using his old name, Jacob, as you do with an old acquaintance. He promised His personal presence for this next and final move and even told Jacob that Joseph would take care of his body when he died. The journey of a leader or any man or woman with God is *all the way*, and this final touching vision summarizes the principle well. Jacob had come to a time in his life when he could say wherever, whatever and however to God's call.

So Israel set out with all that he had, and came to Beersheba, and offered sacrifices to the God of his father Isaac. God spoke to Israel in visions of the night and said, "Jacob, Jacob." And he said, "Here I am." He said, "I am God, the God of your father; do not be afraid to go down to Egypt, for I will make you a great nation there. I will go down with you to Egypt, and I will also surely bring you up again; and Joseph will close your eyes" (Genesis 46:1-4).

In this final recorded personal communication to Jacob, it was just like old times when God said, "Jacob, Jacob," and now Jacob could respond to an intensely loved and respected friend by saying, "Here I am." In this case, he was setting out toward Egypt via Beersheba, to leave the land where his heart always was, but God's final promise included a return clause for a final burial back there! Having a relationship with God like Jacob did will bring comfort to us as we live toward the final years of our lives, when the things that have meant so much to us begin to be stripped away.

Sometimes I find the idea of going all the way with God frightening. But a developing *Integration Quotient* means I must be willing to surrender my reservations.

**Waiting Well!**

What people blurt out is often indicative of what is deeply embedded in their hearts. When Billy Graham spoke to a private gathering at Gordon-Conwell Seminary, he suddenly said, "I don't know why the Lord chose me for what He gave me to do." In my mother's final days, during a conversation around the table, she unexpectedly said, "I am going to pray for grace to leave this world with dignity." Both of these statements come from deep within. Very late in Jacob's life, he too made a sudden statement that epitomized his life.

Right in the middle of the blessings he was giving his sons, he said, "For Your salvation I wait, O Lord" (Genesis 49:18). What could be going on in his mind? Proceeding through the names of his sons, he could not help but be reminded of his very dangerous journey. He had mentioned Simeon and Levi early, and they may have triggered his outburst. By massacring the Shechemites, they could have been responsible for the slaughter of his entire family if surrounding tribes had taken vengeance quickly enough.

In the Old Testament, the concept of *salvation* is weighted toward deliverance. Jacob had waited on the Lord for deliverance time after time ever since he left home. There was a period of several years in my own experience in which I said almost reflexively, "Lord, I am waiting." One of the thoughts closest to Jacob's heart was God's salvation or deliverance during his life. You can see a similar strain in Celtic prayers. They lived in such a dangerous era that being able to survive or gain protection from God was basic in their praying.

Like the Apostle who had more in mind than just living longer, when he mentioned God's deliverance or salvation in Philippians 1:19-20, so Jacob's sudden exclamation about waiting on God's salvation extended to the totality of his life experience. Leaders who spend a lifetime waiting on God will experience deliverance and more–life formation which is significant, lasting, and meaningful.

Leaders who spend their lives attempting to find every resource to survive and win but fail to wait on God's deliverance or salvation, are missing more than they realize. Like Jacob, they need to be able to say after they have fought, survived, and won, "I have waited for Thy salvation, O Lord." This attitude of waiting on God positions us in an inner place where God is recognized as our Provider, Deliverer, Guide–our ultimate expectation.

**Finally**

We have selected a few of the incidents in Jacob's life to say one thing in this chapter. A healthy *Integration Quotient* comes as the result of *a developing and deepening relationship with God for the entirety of our life while experiencing God's deliverance to make it happen.* We too are called to the long journey of an interconnected life with the Lord.

THE LEADER'S JOURNEY. . .
**Gaining a growing maturing relationship
with God which impacts the lives of others
as a net result of life experience**

Questions for Reflection (alone or in a group):

1. Like Jacob at Peniel, are you able to be transparent with God so that you are not hiding anything?

2. As you have considered Jacob's progress after his exile, do you see parallels in your own life?

3. To what extent do you have an emerging life with God?

4. Are you inspired in some way as you consider this chapter? How?

5. What can you implement into your own life from this chapter? Are you planning to "get clean" in some way or making a decision to work on an aspect of your life?

**Response**

Prayer for a developing relationship with God in which you respond progressively.

# PART TWO

# ARRIVING

# CHAPTER 13

# LEADERS –
# AND THOSE THEY LOVE?

*Home is a mighty test of character.*
*What you are at home you are everywhere,*
*whether you demonstrate it or not.*
                    *Thomas De Witt Talmage*

*And Leah's eyes were weak, but Rachel was beautiful of*
*form and face. Now Jacob loved Rachel, so he said, "I will*
*serve you seven years for your younger daughter Rachel."*
*So Jacob served seven years for Rachel and they seemed to*
*him but a few days because of his love for her. So Jacob...*
*loved Rachel more than Leah.*
                    *Genesis 29:17, 18, 20, 30*

*All the people who were in the court, and the elders, said,*
*"We are witnesses, May the LORD make the woman who is*
*coming into your home like Rachel and Leah, both of whom*
*built the house of Israel."*
                    *Ruth 4:11*

*One of the marks of true greatness
is the ability to develop greatness in others.*
                                    *J. C. Macaulay*

# LEADERS – AND THOSE THEY LOVE?

Why a question mark to begin this chapter? Don't leaders love? Can they love? Of course they can, but many don't. Some have a tendency toward narcissism (even the occasional pastor!) with personalities characterized by emotional difficulty or inability to love someone outside themselves. Others find it hard to let others into their world unless they revolve around their own interests. Others mortgage relationships with those closest to them to follow their vision in leading a company, organization or church. Perhaps you know a leader who is disconnected from loved ones, or perhaps you have been that person yourself.

In my first meeting with Jan, I was impressed that he was a leader who had learned to love. His manufacturing business had tripled during the calendar year when a major client moved its operations to the Chicago area. In spite of the stress this was causing, he made a costly commitment to his wife that he would be home by 6:00 each evening.

He had been recently selected to lead a ministry in a mega-church, and he was preparing to conduct a retreat for spouses because he felt his leadership would be a failure if he didn't strengthen the marriages of those he was leading. His own journey as a leader who knew how to love had not been an easy one.

A few years back, his wife took the children back to their home country. He said, "My wife is high maintenance. She needs to be treated like a queen." While she was out of the country, he met a woman who felt that a man should be treated like a king and treated him like one. He was magnetized, and this woman became his mistress temporarily.

His comments now communicate that he not only loves his wife but is also in love with her, and he noted enthusiastically how she is growing as a wife and person. These are the elements that we look at more deeply in Jacob's experience.

Leaders we have followed while exploring Jacob's life express concern over this core of loving in the primary relationships of their lives, particularly their spouses. Sometimes we meet together with the spouse and go through a survey they answer individually with questions about level of fulfillment, whether the business is the right platform for one or both of their lives, and whether or not growth spiritually and personally is being encouraged.

I do not know how the answers to these types of questions would have been articulated in Jacob's household. We do know that he found himself in a situation that would have given men in his culture a license to harm those closest to him. We have already noted how Jacob dreamed of marrying Rachel from the first time he met her and slaved for seven years for the privilege to do so. Yet his father-in-law, Laban, foisted Leah, the older and less desirable daughter, on Jacob when he thought he was getting Rachel. You can imagine Leah's situation–as the possible target for Jacob's blistering anger and rage that he couldn't take out on his father-in-law!

Jacob then promised Laban that if he would work another seven years, he would give Rachel to him in marriage. Laban agreed and immediately Jacob found himself with a second wife. This senario set up Leah for a level of unhappiness that we find in today's soap operas. Jacob's marriage to the two sisters gives us the opportunity to ask, "How well did Jacob love his wives?" Even more pointed is the question, "Did both Leah and Rachel find fulfillment and opportunities to develop their own lives as a result of the way Jacob treated them?"

Few individuals or families face more difficulties than Jacob did. Yet what we learn from Jacob's convoluted marital, home and family situation gives us three principles about the way leaders must relate to their mates. If you find yourself in a difficult marriage, or even in love with someone other than your mate, these principles will help you navigate the troublesome waters of your marriage. Even if you find it virtually impossible to emotionally engage your mate at a deep and meaningful level, there is something to be learned from the life of Jacob. After all, he ended up with one wife he did not want and one he was in love with all his life (not to mention two servant women who bore him children)! Jacob succeeded with those closest to him even though he lived through the trauma of thirteen children born of four women, his only daughter raped, his oldest son guilty of incest, and his favorite son sold into slavery by his brothers. How did he manage in spite of his circumstances?

### Providing a *P l a c e*

Leah is a classic example of the *unloved wife*. She was more homely than her sister, Rachel. Her eyes were weak and she lacked the flashing beauty that Middle Eastern women prize. The fact that she was not already married when Jacob showed up suggests that she was not very good marriage material.

Rachel, on the other hand, was *Miss Universe*. When Leah was imposed on Jacob on his wedding night, only the most naive would expect Jacob to say, "I'll be as happy with Leah as I would have been with Rachel." He was heartbroken over his marriage to Leah, and so was Rachel. A built-in conflict is established between the two sister-wives. The Hebrew word for a second wife meant *rival* (Herbert, p. 87).

In spite of the fact that Leah and her servant woman gave birth to the majority of the twelve patriarchal heads of the nation of Israel (six from Leah and two from Zilpah), her name is mentioned fewer than forty times in the Old Testament. She is named only once outside of Genesis, and in the twenty-six verses describing the rapid birth of Jacob's children, the problem of not being loved by her husband is mentioned in one way or another *eight times!* Leah was not ready to step back as the unloved wife who was grateful just to have a husband in a culture where her existence depended on a man. She cried out for what any woman wants–love and acceptance from her husband, a place in his heart. She was consumed with the desire to be loved, accepted and cherished by Jacob.

Though Jacob did not love Leah as he did Rachel, there is no evidence that he refused to give her a rightful place in his home. When it was time to make his break with Laban, he called both Rachel *and* Leah for this family council, and they spoke as equals in the decision to leave their father (Genesis 31:4, 14). Rachel and Leah are mentioned equally as his wives during the crisis with Esau (32:22-23; 33:1-2). Leah had access to Jacob's bed, and both she and Zilpah had children by him. He didn't take another beautiful woman like Rachel and abandon Leah, or reduce her status to that of a demeaned household slave when it could have been his cultural right to do so.

Years later, Joseph had a dream about an amazing level of supremacy he would have over every member of Jacob's family. This was hard even for his doting father to swallow, and Jacob replied, "Shall I and *your mother* . . . bow ourselves to the ground before you?" Leah was *not* Joseph's mother; Rachel was, but she was dead. Why then did Jacob call Leah *your mother*? She now had a full and honored status in the home. We don't know how close she was to Jacob's heart, but they were together in a meaningful and real way.

The first principle to be seen and applied by a leader toward his or her mate is one of true recognition and respect. Jacob gave Leah a meaningful *place* in his life even though she was not his first choice. She was valued as a person in her own right in a culture that gave Jacob great latitude in how he treated her.

## A Place to *D e v e l o p*

Rachel got what only a few women get in life–a man who was passionately and permanently in love with her to the extent that he never got over her death. Her son Joseph was Jacob's favorite just because he was Rachel's firstborn. Leah didn't enjoy this level of affection from Jacob. Yet there was something that both Rachel and Leah received from Jacob that proved to be far more important than either of their emotional experiences with him. They were given a place to *develop* with Jacob.

There is a mysterious statement in the New Testament concerning women which reads, "She will be saved through childbearing–if she continues in faith and love and holiness and self-control" (1 Timothy 2:15). In a strangely remarkable way, both Rachel and Leah were *saved through childbearing* in terms of their spiritual development with Jacob. This is how it happened.

Rachel and Leah lived in their father's mean-spirited pagan home. Laban's vision for life restricted all who were close to him. It is little wonder then that his two daughters were willing to turn their backs on their family of origin and never look back. They knew there was nothing left for them there (Genesis 31:14-16). However, Rachel couldn't leave behind her father's household gods. They were necessary to her sense of well-being as she left what she would never see again.

Like many of Solomon's wives and concubines, Leah and Rachel could have been untouched by Jacob's faith and knowledge of God. Instead, both women came to a deep and abiding faith in the true God through their birthing and family experiences.

The pivotal saga of the birth of Jacob's children is told in Genesis 29:31-30:24. The spotlight was immediately on Leah before any of the children were born. "Now the LORD saw that Leah was unloved, and He opened her womb, but

Rachel was barren" (29:31). The term *LORD* is used since this designation implies His personal revelation and relationship (the idea is developed fully in Exodus 3). God was building a relationship with Leah! This was a result of living with Jacob.

When Leah was honored with Reuben, the firstborn of Jacob's family, she responded, "Because the LORD has seen my affliction, surely now my husband will love me" (29:32). She got the message of a revealing God who wanted a relationship with her even when her husband didn't! She had already developed far beyond where she would have ever been in her own home.

After another son, Simeon, was born, she said, "Because the LORD has heard that I am unloved, He has therefore given me this son also" (29:33). Do you remember how God intervened for Jacob in his career? He was doing the same thing with Leah! It was Jacob against Laban, and now it was Leah in her career as a wife and mother vying for the love of her husband. God was on her side like He was with Jacob! Think of what life might have been like for this physically flawed woman in Laban's pagan household–no knowledge of God and maybe pawned off on one of the most undesirable men in the region for a permanently miserable life. But in Jacob's household, things were very different for Leah.

When son number three was born Leah responded by saying, "Now this time my husband will become attached to me, because I have borne him three sons" (29:34). Leah was coming into her own, her confidence building. Son number four caused Leah to celebrate, "This time I will praise the LORD" (29:35). No longer focusing on the heady experience of having the great God, the LORD, help her bear children to get the love of her husband, she simply said, "I will praise the LORD." She was developing her own relationship with God.

The same was true of Rachel. She was the last to have a baby (Leah, Bilhah and Zilpah all preceded her), but when she finally conceived, she moved from serving her father's pagan idols to loving the God of Jacob. The text is plain that God intervened on Rachel's behalf and that she then learned to address the God of the universe and receive an answer.

> Then God remembered Rachel, and God gave heed to her and opened her womb. So she conceived and bore a son and said, "God has taken away my reproach." She named him Joseph, saying, "May the LORD give me another son!" (30:22-24)

She gave God credit for taking away her reproach of being childless. She expressed confidence that the LORD (the God who had become personal to her) would grant her another son. She was absolutely and tragically right. The next son would be extraordinarily important in the plan of God, but would cost her life and make her a leading character in one of the great love tragedies in literature. A final development scene involved the entire family.

> God said to Jacob, "Arise, go up to Bethel and live there, and make an altar there to God, who appeared to you when you fled from your brother Esau." So Jacob said to his household and all who were with him, "Put away the foreign gods which are among you, and purify yourselves and change your garments; and let us arise and go up to Bethel, and I will make an altar there to God, who answered me in the day of my distress and has been with me wherever I have gone." *So they gave to Jacob all the foreign gods which they had and the rings that were in their ears, and Jacob hid them under the oak which was near Shechem.* As they journeyed, there was a great terror upon the cities which were around them, and they did not pursue the sons of Jacob (35:1-5, italics mine).

God was helping this family and clan develop. With the call to return to Bethel, what Jacob experienced alone was now to be reenacted with everyone present as Jacob called for an act of cleansing. It was a complete break with all foreign gods, even earrings which reminded his wives of their former gods! Clean clothes were symbolic of this new start. Everything from their pagan past was buried.

God ratified what they did and gave them another object lesson related to their greatest life need at the time–protection. He caused terror to fall on their potential enemies as they traveled safely to Bethel.

Through their interaction with their husband, both Leah and Rachel turned from their father's idols and came to love and worship the God of Abraham, Isaac and Jacob.

## A Place to Find Their *D e s t i n y*

Rachel's first son, Joseph, was a balm to Jacob's heart even though he already had ten sons and a daughter. Jacob's connection with Joseph turned out to be for good reason. Joseph became the vice-regent of Egypt and kept Jacob's entire clan alive during a severe famine. As the mother of Joseph, Rachel is enshrined in history, sharing his astonishing life and career which is significant even today.

When Rachel gave birth to Benjamin and died in the process, she was linked forever in a special way to the coming Messiah. Jeremiah 31:15 speaks of Rachel weeping for her children and refusing all comfort. The prophetic element was fulfilled when Herod massacred the Bethlehem babies under two years of age after Jesus' birth. Rachel's experience was the expression of utter desolation the mothers experienced. "A voice was heard in Ramah, weeping and great mourning, Rachel weeping for her children; and she refused to be comforted, because they were no more" (Matthew 2:18). It was beautiful Rachel's destiny to become a symbol of the tragedy befalling her descendants.

Through the line established by Rachel's son Benjamin came the Apostle Paul who wrote thirteen books of the Bible! Even though she died prematurely, Rachel's life with Jacob gave her a *destiny* for the ages. Like Rachel, Leah became an extraordinary woman of destiny through her sons. Levi's descendants were the priests of the Hebrew theocracy. The temple and rituals they managed point with amazing accuracy in type to Jesus. Judah was the tribe from which Jesus came, as a descendant of David. In this way Leah's sons and their descendants were contributors to the redemptive work of God for the human race.

There is a final and more personal touch in Leah's experience. In Genesis 30:13 she said, "Happy am I! For women will call me happy." Sometimes our desires that well up deep within us are fulfilled and amplified by God to an extent we never believed possible. I think this happened to Leah. She wanted to be remembered favorably by those who followed. We read the amazing fulfillment of wounded Leah's desire in Ruth 4:11 when well wishers were congratulating Boaz on his marriage to Ruth: "May the LORD make the woman, who is coming into your house, like Rachel and Leah who together built up the house of Israel." There it is–Leah as the epitome of blessing along with Rachel. She was fully equal with Rachel as a builder of the nation of Israel, and Jacob was pivotal in helping both women understand and fulfill their destiny.

### Finally

As a leader, you will eventually be judged not only for what you do publicly but also for what you provide for those you are supposed to love. Jacob replaces the question mark about a leader being able to love with an exclamation point when you consider the total environment and times in which he lived. He provided a *place* for his family and helped them *develop* and find their *destinies.*

THE LEADER'S JOURNEY . . .
## Providing a *place* for those you love to *develop* and discover their *destinies*

Questions for Reflection (alone or in a group):

1. How do you react to this chapter? Do you feel encouragement that you are doing what you can for your loved ones, or grief over what is broken and you can't fix?

2. What comes across most clearly to you in this chapter about leaders and their loved ones?

3. In what way(s) might the principles from this chapter contribute to the way you look at your role in life as a leader?

4. What would you most like to communicate to someone else who is leading strongly in public but weakly at home?

5. Is there any action step you would like to take after considering this chapter on leaders and those they love?

6. Are you helping those you love grapple with the big issues and values related to their own destinies?

## Response

Prayer that you will be who and what you can be in your primary relationships so that each person has a place to develop and to move toward their destinies because of you.

# CHAPTER 14

# WHEN LEADERS GRIEVE THEIR LOSSES

*Many of life's disappointments are like rivers without bridges. To get on with your life, you have to take the plunge and swim to the other side. Knowing how to grieve your losses, how to say good-bye to that which will not come about, is a crucial step to wholeness and freedom from unnecessary depression.*

*Archibald D. Hart*

*So Jacob said to Pharaoh, "The years of my sojourning are one hundred and thirty; few and unpleasant have been the years of my life, nor have they attained the years that my fathers lived during the days of their sojourning."*

*Genesis 47:9*

*Great grief makes sacred those upon whom its hand is laid.*
*Joy may elevate,*
*ambition glorify,*
*but only sorrow can consecrate.*

*Horace Greeley*

# WHEN LEADERS GRIEVE THEIR LOSSES

You may remember Preston who listed "woundedness" high on his self-evaluation even though he owned a world-class business. He brought hurt and distress into his professional life from his childhood in a deeply dysfunctional and alcoholic home where he eventually sued for custody of his younger siblings. Yet over the years he never took time or recognized his need to grieve his losses. Perhaps it was because he became very successful in business and helped launch his siblings into their adult lives. Perhaps it was because he was married to his college sweetheart and found pleasure as a devoted father.

Many months after we began meeting, he shared a deeply personal and painful memory with me. His oldest son, to whom he was particularly close, was not his oldest child. His first child had been aborted when his college love became pregnant. They had followed the counsel of someone who supposedly knew best how to handle the situation. Years later when Preston realized his need for some closure, he wrote one of the most touching letters to his unborn child that I have ever read. Preston did his very difficult work and is now living out a freedom which would have been unavailable to him, had he not pushed through his wrenching process. As a result, he can reach out to others who have this same heartbreak.

Leaders need to grieve their losses at some point. By the time they reach their fifties, they usually have deep wounds from difficult life experiences. Some plunge into grief when they realize that while succeeding in business, they have forfeited their relationship with a mate or children. Some feel great pain from the wound of trusted friends or associates who turned against them out of jealousy or greed. Some live with the scenario of "what might have been" after giving everything they had to develop a business, only to see their life's efforts and investments come to nothing.

If you have suffered losses, this chapter is for you! From the life of Jacob we will discover the work which must be done in order to grieve losses in a healthy way and move forward in life. If we have not grieved our losses well, we keep ourselves from living with inward wholeness. We prevent ourselves from being completely human.

Jacob's experience 4,000 years ago is a compelling example for leaders today. His life of conflict was foreshadowed in his struggle with Esau in their mother's womb. It's as if Jacob was teed up to get smacked!

Jacob was hit off the tee when Esau made plans to kill him. He rolled down the hill to a hard life in his exile years in Syria slaving for his father-in-law, Laban. Jacob held his life together, gritted his teeth and served another seven years after Laban switched Leah for Rachel.

He made the best of his chance to go on his own instead of continuing as a hired hand for Laban while his cousins got preferential treatment. Twenty years of hard living required him to be strong, keep up a good appearance and push on. When a wise woman told me, "You have comforted others and been strong for them; you need comfort yourself," she no doubt could have said the same thing to Jacob. He was living without a lot of nurture and comfort while he was being treated badly year after year.

Jacob finally went after Laban with a dramatic verbal assault as he was leaving his abusive father-in-law (Genesis 31:25-42). The essence of what he had to say can be summarized this way: "I suffered badly in the twenty years I've been with you. You never treated me fairly or even decently. You changed my wages downward at least ten times and did everything you could to sabotage me. Even now, you would send me away with nothing if you could. I married your daughters under the most difficult circumstances, and there has never been a day I have not been faithful to them or taken care of them in a way that is honorable. Toward me, you have no heart. I am less than nothing to you."

Jacob never again seemed to possess the same vigor and strength he had during his exile period with Laban. He was on his way to becoming a man who bore the "searing wound" that can make or break a leader.

**Wounded Warrior**

When Jacob returned to his homeland, he faced another hurdle with his brother. He could not assume Esau would be friendly toward him after all these years of separation. The night before their encounter was the worst single night of Jacob's life. Though it proved to be a night of transformation, he paid a high price by limping the rest of his life.

One never fully recovers from any terrible, full-blown crisis. A Latvian ichthyologist escaped the communists who took over his country and told of experiences from which he never recovered. "It was like my nerves were being snapped one by one." Jacob received the sledgehammer blow that led to the defining moment of his life at Peniel, but it also left him crippled. A tremendous accumulation of difficult experiences often leaves a leader wounded and grieving. Times like this remind me of a comment made by Chris Carmichael, Lance Armstrong's trainer for his multiple Tour de France wins. He said that one never fully recovers from *one* Tour de France!

Events continued to pile up in Jacob's household. When Leah's daughter, Dinah, visited another clan, the sheik's son, Shechem, forced her to bed with him (Genesis 34). Although he loved her and wished to marry her, Dinah's brothers, Simeon and Levi, massacred the men of the sheik's village in retaliation. Now Jacob's household was in danger of being wiped out. His response to his sons' actions seems self-centered in that Jacob used "me, my, and I" seven times in the one verse (34:30). Perhaps he was turning inward as a result of the stress that had come from so many directions.

When the family arrived in Bethlehem (a suburb of Jerusalem today), Rachel died giving birth to Benjamin. She was the supreme love of his life, and he never recovered. At the end of his life, he still mourned her death and reminisced sadly before blessing her grandsons, Ephraim and Manasseh (Genesis 48). Genesis 35 also records the death of his father, Isaac. During Jacob's time of grief, his oldest son, Reuben, slept with Bilhah, Rachel's maid.

**Nonstop Grief**

Jacob was more deeply attached to Rachel's sons, Joseph and Benjamin, than to any of his other children. In a jealous rage his older sons sold Joseph to slave traders heading for Egypt and then deceived their father into thinking Joseph was dead. It seemed more than he could handle:

> So Jacob tore his clothes, and put sackcloth on his loins and mourned for his son many days. Then all his sons and all his daughters arose to comfort him, but he refused to be comforted. And he said, "Surely I will go down to Sheol in mourning for my son." So his father wept for him (Genesis 37:34-35).

For Jacob it was nonstop pain. Rachel, the love of his life, was dead. His mother, Rebekah, had died without a good-bye from her son. Joseph was dead as far as Jacob was concerned. Benjamin would soon be forced to go to Egypt in order for the clan to have food during a famine, only to be held hostage as a test of the integrity of his brothers. With the seizing of Benjamin his brothers pled for mercy on the basis that Jacob's "life is bound up in the boy's life. As soon as he sees that the boy is not with us, he will die, and your servants will bring down the gray hairs of your servant our father with sorrow to Sheol" (44:31).

## Jacob's Anguish in Pharaoh's Presence

When we add up the events we have catalogued from Jacob's twenty years in Syria until his journey to Egypt, it is no wonder that his response to Pharaoh's question about his age caused him to emphasize his grief.

Pharaoh said to Jacob, "How many years have you lived?" So Jacob said to Pharaoh, "The years of my sojourning are one hundred and thirty; few and unpleasant have been the years of my life, nor have they attained the years that my fathers lived during the days of their sojourning" (Genesis 47:8-9).

While he might have given testimony to God's power in his life or told events from his incredible life, what we find is Jacob expressing his profoundly felt woe. He evaluated his life as *evil*, a Hebrew word that can be translated *wretched* or *unhappy*.

## No Such Thing as a Surface Wound

You may be disappointed with Jacob's response to his troubled life. Indeed, his life was often chaotic and troubled, and he reacted as the wounded man he was. Yet the great reality that pervaded his life was the presence of God and the assigned plan that he never lost sight of.

Are your wounds still affecting you? You can use heartbreaks to open doors for healing and wholeness. Much of the book of Job is taken up with his grieving process. We also have the example of Hannah who poured out her heart in wrenching pain over her barren condition (1 Samuel 1). The Apostle Paul suffered terrible loss but faced it squarely and spoke out of a new reality when he said, "I count everything to be loss in view of the surpassing value of knowing Christ Jesus my Lord, for whom *I have suffered the loss of all things* [italics mine], and count them but rubbish so that I may gain Christ (Philippians 3:8).

You may feel a need to make use of additional resources. In *Unmasking Male Depression*, Archibald D. Hart writes of the losses which precipitate grieving and offers several steps toward making this a constructive process. For example, the loss must be identified and understood instead of being permitted to float around like some amorphous mass. This involves separating abstract or imagined losses from real losses. The grieving process must be facilitated, permitted to happen. We must face the reality of the loss and let it go. Only then are we ready to develop a perspective for the loss (pp.151-157).

Sometimes we feel embarrassed about hurting over a loss when others have lost more. Our griefs are still ours even though someone else might handle them differently. Gavin expressed his deep anger in a retreat setting and was rebuked sharply for being so upset when others had much more difficult lives. "Their difficult circumstances don't help me," he said. He could have quoted Shakespeare, "Every one can master a grief but he that hath it." He still hadn't worked through his own grief and disappointment with how his life was turning out.

I remember praying at one point, "Lord, I understand that I am grieving, but I don't know how to stop it." Whatever the time frame, Cicero's insight is comforting–"No grief is so acute but that time ameliorates it." We can't suggest a time frame for Jacob, since he grieved and continued to experience more reasons to grieve. Your situation may be similar, but you can push on through this cycle like Jacob and innumerable others have done.

Jacob took hits in his life that could have destroyed him. He grieved his losses, survived them and moved forward with his life. His final years are a powerful climax for a man who had lost so much along the way. Like Jacob, you can travel beyond your brokenness and wounds and live the remainder of your life in a positive and fulfilling way. Have you given yourself permission to grieve the losses you have experienced?

THE LEADER'S JOURNEY . . .

**Honest encounters with your grief or wounds and . . .**

**Finding your way through grief to live with God and others more deeply**

Questions for Reflection (alone or in a group):

1. Has your life so far been unscathed by grief or sorrow? If not, have you been able to voice your pain in a helpful manner or are you still in a cover-up mode?

2. Who would be able to listen without trying to fix you? Have you ever had a conversation with someone like that?

3. We don't know how much comfort Jacob received from a human source, but what might you have wanted to do if you had a meaningful friendship with him?

4. How have you coped with the pain or grief you have experienced? Do you think you have come through well?

**Response**

Prayer that you will accept your losses and grieve if necessary, so that you do not live with unresolved issues such as bitterness or exaggerated sense of loss.

# CHAPTER 15

# THE POWER TO BLESS

＋══╪

*Leaders can be, when they choose,
significant bearers of gifts to the spirit.*

*Max DePree*

*Then Joseph brought his father Jacob and presented him to
Pharaoh; and Jacob blessed Pharaoh.*

*Genesis 47:7*

*There are persons about whom one senses wisdom, a depth,
a wealth of experience, a center forged deeply by life.
Educated or uneducated, such persons seem to possess
a sacred place within them, where they have pondered.
We sense that somehow they know,
whatever that might mean.
And no matter how much they might share,
there always seems
to be more at a depth that cannot be emptied.
And so, rather than try, one is sometimes content
simply to be in their presence.*

*W. Paul Jones*

# THE POWER TO BLESS

Some leaders have *the power to bless*–the intangible ability to impact, inspire, influence or contribute to the lives of others because of who they are and what they have become. The *power to bless* is an important aspect of a true leader. At an important juncture in Jacob's life, this quality surfaced in a powerful way.

What does this quality look like in the life of today's leader? In considering this question I could not help but think of Jackson, a man who headed up a company whose revenues exceed $100 million per year. He was unusually influential, but he did not confuse his business platform with who he was as a person. He refused to use his influence to gain personal advantage and was intentional in staying quietly behind the scenes, being warm and supportive to those who came to him for advice.

In one of our conversations Jackson spoke of the life principles he had learned from the founding members of the family business. As he spoke, what was most evident to me was how his faith and commitment to God clearly set his core values and agenda. Instead of seeking to make yet more money and become more successful, Jackson focused his life on things that matter far more than dollars. Somehow, he made me want to live my life on a higher plane.

Because of who Jackson is and what he has become, those with whom he comes in contact find their lives enriched. Jackson is able to maximize his impact on others because he models what we instinctively know is real success instead of the nonessential trappings that we also know are not really important.

The film *Chariots of Fire* captured a similar situation. The film relates the story of Eric Liddell who refused to compromise his conviction about running on Sunday during the 1924 Olympics. His future king defended Eric to the

Olympic committee by observing that Eric's ability to run was an extension of who he was. Forcing him to run on Sunday would violate Eric's integrity and make him average instead of world class.

The power to bless because of who one is and what one has become is the principle we are considering in Jacob's life. His power to bless as a leader was the result of who he had become, and a single incident later in his life sums up this result.

### Jacob's Power to Bless Pharaoh

A famine in Canaan forced Jacob to move to Egypt where he was reunited with Joseph. Necessary protocol involved a meeting with Pharaoh before the family reaped the benefits of the generosity that Joseph earned for them. When Jacob stood before Pharaoh because of his son's influence, he was a most unlikely candidate to bless or contribute something to one of the most powerful men in his ancient world. Severe famine had made him a refugee in Egypt. He was also a shepherd, and shepherds had no status among the Egyptians.

Pharaoh was ruler of the greatest nation in the world at that time, and Jacob at best was similar to a local sheik. Pharaoh ruled a great land that stretched along the Nile for hundreds of miles. Jacob owned nothing except the bit of land he purchased when he briefly stayed in Shechem. Pharaoh was an automatic choice for any register of the famous and powerful, while Jacob was a candidate for a great unknown of his day–at least, in Egypt.

With courageous openness with the Pharaoh, Jacob permitted his grief to surface while speaking about his troubled life. Ordinarily, Pharaoh might have brushed off people like this. Yet Jacob blessed Pharaoh twice (Genesis 47:7, 10).

Why did he have the audacity, authority, ability and authenticity to bless a great leader like the Pharaoh? The universally held principle is that "the inferior is blessed by the superior," as in the case of Melchizedek, king of Salem and priest of God, who blessed Abraham (Hebrews 7:4-10).

Was Jacob as an old man thinking he was more than he was, or was he in touch with something powerfully true about himself? At least one commentator suggests that his son Joseph sensed this special quality before he placed his father before Pharaoh. He had the *power to bless* with a certain self-authentication that made the external qualifications he lacked unnecessary. We don't know the content of Jacob's blessing or whether he brought Pharaoh to God in a priestly role. We simply know that Jacob blessed the Pharaoh, providing a special elevating experience for this great man.

How is it that Jacob had this authority and authenticity to bless? Two characteristics show us how and why Jacob was able to bless the Pharaoh.

*A purposeful life.* Jacob was living according to a *call* that God placed on his life. A *call* in life invariably involves some kind of *plan*. One element of the *plan* in the Abrahamic Covenant was that "in you all the families of the earth shall be blessed"(Genesis12:3). This blessing of Jacob on Pharaoh was an early note in this symphony of blessing which is still being played out today. Jacob was doing what his descendants were going to do in far greater ways throughout the centuries to follow.

In the covenant promise to Abraham (Genesis 15:13, 18), God informed Abraham that his descendants would be sojourners for 400 years before inheriting the Promised Land. Abraham's grandson Jacob was standing before Pharaoh and initiating this 400-year period with a blessing on the sovereign monarch of Egypt.

If you are living out a *call* and *plan* for your life, you are probably finding that the *power to bless* and make a difference in people's lives happens when it is least expected. One of these unanticipated incidents occurred for me before sunrise in a Florida coffee shop on the intercoastal waterway. Seeing my open Bible, Jack asked what I was reading. Almost instantly we launched a life-changing relationship. As a fugitive from the pastorate, he was living with the financial struggles of a new real estate career (his water had been shut off once during this time). We struck up a significant friendship. When we met a couple of years later at the same coffee shop, he had become the lead teacher in a real estate school and was weeks away from launching his own brokerage and real estate investment business. He mentioned repeatedly that our relationship was critical in helping him move through a difficult period of his life. With Jack I experienced what is one of the most meaningful and powerfully motivating aspects of my life–*the power to bless.*

*Woundedness.* The second factor that contributed to Jacob's ability to bless is, on first glance, rather surprising. Yet the power to bless always comes from an authentic place in one's soul, and authenticity is often formed by personal difficulties and tragedies. The late Henri Nouwen penned the phrase *wounded healers* to describe those who bless because of what they have survived. Like Jacob, wounded healers have had a crucible experience that purified or prepared them. When leaders experience wounding or intense ordeals, they are pushed to the essential core of their lives.

It is very doubtful that Jacob would have had the authority to bless Pharaoh as he did without the afflictions which hammered him so many years. His crushing crisis transformation at Peniel, leaving him with a limp the rest of his life, was part of the price he paid for his authenticity and his ability to bless. By following Jacob's life to this point, we understand that his development and spiritual formation helped to make him the man who was able to bless Pharaoh. Are you aware of a similar process in your own life that is causing you to be able to impact the lives of others, sometimes in unexpected, unanticipated instances?

## Jacob's Power to Bless His Sons and Grandsons

Jacob clearly had the power to bless because of who he was and what he had become, and his most significant blessing involved his sons and grandsons. It is such a powerful blessing that it makes the New Testament's *Hall of Faith* list–Hebrews 11:21: "By faith Jacob, as he was dying, blessed each of the sons of Joseph."

The blessing given by Jacob to his sons and grandsons is instructive as to the nature of a true and rich blessing. There are three aspects which point us toward the character of the blessings we want to receive as well as the ones we need to give.

*The leader's blessing is discerning and perceptive.* Jacob's striking and markedly prophetic blessing on his sons was not only suited to each but deeply discerning. Reuben was the first to receive Jacob's pronouncement. Jacob blessed and honored him not only in the context of being the firstborn but reduced what he might have expected in view of his immorality with Bilhah, Rachel's maid. He proceeded to bless each son, censoring some, using vivid descriptions with all, and looking down the corridor of time to the future roles their descendants would fill. Judah and Joseph were given the longest blessings and have had the greatest historical and spiritual importance to future believers (Genesis 49:8-12, 22-26). Joseph, who suffered the most, was given a blessing six times in two of the verses devoted to him.

Jacob had the power to bless his sons with a blessing suitable for each one! The net result of Jacob's blessing is summarized as follows: "All these are the twelve tribes of Israel. This is what their father said to them as he *blessed* them, *blessing* each with the *blessing suitable to him* (Genesis 49:28, italics mine). Leaders with *the power to bless are discerning.* Their blessings are not thrown like mud on the wall to see what sticks and what doesn't. What they convey is not sloppy, slushy or sentimental, but like the deliberate shooting of an arrow to a target.

Jacob's blessing of his family members is also prophetic and absolute. His discernment was unerring when he blessed Manasseh and Ephraim, the sons of Joseph. Joseph corrected Jacob's apparent mistake of placing his right hand on the youngest when Jacob gave the two boys his blessing. It was not because of Jacob's age or failing eyesight that be blessed younger Ephraim over older Manasseh. His viewpoint was prophetic. Precisely as his blessing indicated, Ephraim became the most prominent among Jacob's descendants, and sometimes the whole nation of Israel was referred to as *Ephraim* (see Genesis 48:9-20).

If we, like Jacob, are living out a plan, engaged in a life of spiritual formation and life development, pushed to the depth of our own souls through crisis and confrontation with God, we will be able to speak to others with insight and influence that affect the rest of their lives.

*Blessing is a result of blessing.* This timeless factor is suggested by the fact that some form of the word *bless* occurs at least fifteen times in Genesis 48–49. Leaders with *the power to bless bless as they have been blessed.* When Jacob left home, Isaac gave his own blessing but also called down the blessing of God Almighty and Abraham on Jacob. At Peniel, Jacob was blessed once when he was heading to Syria and again when he returned to his homeland (32:29; 35:9). *Blessing* was an overriding theme in Jacob's life, and now he blessed because he had been blessed.

In blessing Ephraim and Manasseh, Jacob said, "God Almighty appeared to me at Luz in the land of Canaan and blessed me" (48:3), referring to his Bethel experience. Jacob's blessing on Joseph called God "the Strong One of Jacob" and "the Shepherd of Israel" (49:22-26).

Robert Wicks wrote, "While we are meeting our destiny, others who come into contact with us can embrace their

God-given destiny as well" (p.5). Two thirty-year-old memories persist in my mind as I think about receiving a blessing from others. High in the Rockies at Bear Trap Ranch just after my conversion experience, I was like an absorbent sponge. I don't remember a word the missionary statesman from China said the first evening, but when I looked up at him as he walked to the podium, I saw what I wanted to become.

The other memory comes from the next morning. In the mountain chill I saw Rusty, a red-haired staff member, sitting alone at a picnic table pouring over the Bible. He was encompassed in his own sacred space during his personal meeting with God. It made such an impression on me that over the years I have created my own sacred space hundreds of times in my time with God. The unplanned scene in the flow of camp life, where Rusty was doing what he did and being who he was, is still a part of who I am and has helped set the course of my life.

*Blessing is multigenerational.* The contribution of a leader's *power to bless* cannot be contained in one generation. What Jacob said to his sons looked forward to future generations. For example, his prophetic blessing on Judah contained a reference to the coming Messiah. Jacob's blessing on his grandsons also skipped a generation. When today's leaders have *the power to bless*, their legacy, impact, gifts and contributions reach beyond their own time. Their contribution cannot be contained in one generation.

None of us will have *the power to bless* exactly as Jacob did. Ours will not be as spectacular, prophetic, or precise, but each of us is called upon to be a leader *with the ability to bless powerfully, generously and effectively.* As we do, like Jacob, the results will not be contained in the short time period in which we live.

THE LEADER'S JOURNEY . . .
### Finding the power to bless out of your life and leadership

Questions for Reflection (alone or in a group):

1.  Why is *the power to bless* an important ingredient in the lives of leaders today?

2.  How would you describe the leader's *power to bless?* How does it work?

3.  What is your reaction to this chapter? What is its message to you?

4.  What aspect of Jacob's ability to bless impacted you the most?

5.  Do you have any idea of the blessings that are being called out of your life for others?

**Response**

Prayer for a powerfully developed ability to bless to the extent that you may become a significant influence in the lives of others.

# CHAPTER 16

# CONVERGENCE!

*The trouble with our age is that it is all signposts and no destination.*

*Louis Kronenberger*

*By faith Jacob, as he was dying, blessed each of the sons of Joseph, and worshiped, leaning on the top of his staff.*

*Hebrews 11:21*

*When Jacob finished charging his sons, he drew his feet into the bed and breathed his last, and was gathered to his people.*

*Genesis 49:33*

*Every action taken,*
  *every response made,*
    *every dynamic of relationship,*
      *every thought held,*
        *every emotion allowed:*
      *these are the minuscule arenas where,*
      *bit by bit . . .*
        *we are shaped into some kind of being . . . .*
      *Life is, by its very nature, spiritual formation.*

*M. Robert Mulholland, Jr.*

# CONVERGENCE!

A fter focusing on one aspect of Jacob's journey in each chapter, we now come to the end of his life, not only in terms of his years but more importantly in terms of his development. A term that describes the maturity he has gained through all his ups and downs, all his successes and failures, all his pleasures and pains, is *convergence*.

Convergence should be a holy grail of human experience. The theme of convergence pushed me to reflect on my own life. When I experienced crushing heartbreaks, unbelievable privileges, or shattered dreams, I could embrace the words of the seventeenth-century hymn writer, Joachim Neander, "Hast thou not seen how thy desires e'er have been granted in what He ordaineth?" ("Praise to the Lord, the Almighty," 1680). The equilibrium of convergence, when the deepest desires of the heart coalesce with what God has ordained for one's life, is a stabilizer during our shifting life encounters.

Our study of Jacob's life from womb to tomb reveals a man who came to the point of convergence. This does not mean that Jacob had everything figured out or that all his bitter memories were forgotten. It does not mean that his circumstances were wonderful. What it does mean is that the tangled threads, challenging elements, and stories of his life fit together into a more meaningful whole than he could have imagined while he was working his way through life. We could say Jacob found God, himself, and others. Not a few leaders face the end of their lives with a disconnect from their truest selves, their most important relationships and a developed relationship with God.

Bruce Wilkinson was the first one I heard use the term *convergence* to describe this crucial phase of one's life. In a message entitled, *The Nine Steps from Conversion to Convergence* (FCCI Master's Series), he said that *conver-*

*gence* involves a deep and settled knowledge of why God put you on earth (your life purpose), what your legacy is supposed to be, what your role in life is and how you are to accomplish your life tasks. As you begin this final chapter, do you have an idea of where you would like to be when you are finishing your life or what convergence is supposed to look like for you?

In the introduction I quoted Rabbi Zusya: "In the coming world, they will not ask me; 'Why were you not Moses?' They will ask me; 'Why were you not Zusya?'" Similarly, I cited Elizabeth O'Connor: "If we are to make ultimate sense of our lives, all the disparate elements in us have to be integrated around call." When we experience convergence we are in touch with our "call." When we experience convergence, we are Zusya. Perusing Jacob's life from womb to tomb encourages us to consider how we can be so genuinely who God made us to be that the celebration can be consummated fully only in the next life. He finally arrived where he was supposed to be, not perfectly but, nevertheless, essentially.

The goal for each of us is convergence. It is at the heart of God's plan for us. The process of reaching this is long and arduous, and what the Apostle Paul had in mind when he spoke of the process of "becoming" in Romans 8:29, "For those whom God foreknew, He also predestined *to become* conformed to the image of His Son, so that He would be the firstborn among many brethren." This verse and many others in both Old and New Testaments suggest that God's plan revolves around a process which works in the narrow and sometimes splendid confines of our lives.

The life of Jacob has much to say to today's leaders whose lives are bound to organizational productivity, balance sheets, grueling competition, personnel crises and other issues that spell the difference between the success we seek or the failure we dread. Jacob's life from womb to tomb models this principle of process in which we live with God now to become who we can be.

Convergence means getting where we most need to go in life. Since God has special plans for each person, the process and product for each of us is different in detail but similar in essence. There are three indicators in the story of Jacob that point out how a person can reach his or her life potential. Most likely other elements could be considered signs of a healthy maturity of soul and spirit, but the three we find at the end of Jacob's life are universal in their application.

Perhaps you feel that you are getting a late start on the road to maturity. Take heart! The parable of the workers who were hired late in the day but got the same wages as those who worked all day (Matthew 20:1-16) is a gauge of God's generosity toward us.

### Worship – Maturing with God

The culminating statement about Jacob's life is found in the New Testament. In Hebrews 11:21 we read, "By faith Jacob, when dying, blessed each of the sons of Joseph, *bowing in worship over the head of his staff*" (*italics* mine). Hebrews 11, with its list of those who qualify for the Hall of Faith, underscores the essential spirit of these worthies and greats from the Old Testament, highlighting what God considered most important in their lives. What God wants us to pay particular attention to from the life of Jacob is that he approached death "bowing in worship over the head of his staff." What does this convergent act of Jacob's life mean and what can it teach us?

There is only one prop at this moment and we understand why it is included by looking at Jacob's testimony in Genesis 32:10.

I am unworthy of all the lovingkindness and of all the faithfulness which You have shown to Your servant; for with my staff only I crossed this Jordan, and now I have become two companies.

Jacob's staff is the object which best points to the journey of his life. He carried it from the time he left home until he died. His staff is the tangible object which represents his entire life experience. As he bent over his staff in worship and weakness, he was stating, in a symbolic way, that he was encompassing all his life experience. His worship was not a generous attempt to repay God for a life that went smoothly. He grieved deeply over the tragedies, losses and afflictions that were never far away. However, in the process, he found God in such a way that he could do nothing less than worship. The totality of his life experience led to only one adequate response–bowing in awe. The focus was on his state of being in which his worship indicated the posture of his soul before God.

I am reminded of two personal experiences which help me understand this sacred moment in his life. Jo Ann and I were riding a train in Italy and I walked into a car with open windows and stuck my head out into the brilliant sunshine which lit the Italian countryside and was overwhelmed with the joy of the moment. I prayed immediately, "Lord, as glorious a moment as this is when life can't get much better, without You it would just be another *thing*."

A few years later I was walking a Florida beach on Thanksgiving morning considering the verses which were helping me express my heart to God. Our large family of children, spouses and grandchildren were together for this fantastic week. Psalm 103:1-3 speaks of blessing God and being careful not to forget the blessings He has lavished on us. These moments were suddenly punctuated by the thought, "Lord, You have loaded us with blessings that we might learn to bless You *with or without* the perks or splendid privileges you give!" I was aware that His best blessings are a means of climbing the ladder within to see beyond them to God Himself.

In both of these instances it was impossible for me to give any kind of adequate expression of appreciation or gratitude without moving beyond the blessing to God. Jacob's worship involved moving beyond himself, his life and circumstances to recognize and respond to the glory, greatness and goodness of God. Alfred North Whitehead said, "The worship of God is not a rule of safety–it is an adventure of the spirit." Jacob bargained with God for safety, got it and has now moved on to a higher adventure than merely surviving. Jacob points the way to leaders today. In spite of profound loss, bitter battles and deep woundedness, our lives can become so complete, so developed, that a heart of worship is our instinctive response.

Did Jacob worship using words? When I worked through Psalm 139 with the guidance of a spiritual director, I was so deeply stirred that I made no attempt to verbalize my reaction but simply trusted that God was aware of what I couldn't voice. She responded by telling me about spending thirty-two days with a group of nine women in silence with the result that some of the deepest friendships of her life were formed during this time.

Similarly, Jacob had experienced God in one way or another so long and so often in silence (seemingly endless freezing nights as a shepherd, years of hardship under Laban, separation from his family while working on his family business, having uncertainty and danger as his unwelcome lifelong companion) that it is quite possible words were unnecessary, unwarranted or even inappropriate when *he worshiped God leaning on the top of his staff.* You may have had a similar experience when you went beyond words and worshiped with your being–the inner depths of your person. Worship, whether wordless or not, indicates that the wind of God has blown into your life while you have been journeying to a life summit of convergence!

## Legacy – Fulfilling Your Potential

We all want to make a contribution, leave a legacy or make a difference–mothers in their children, artists in their creations, leaders in their careers or in the entities that survive them. Have you gotten around yet to thinking what you want to leave behind you?

In Genesis 49:29-32 we read what Jacob chose as his final legacy. Surprisingly, it is detailed instructions about his burial place. Notice how specific he is concerning this matter.

> I am about to be gathered to my people; bury me with my fathers in the cave that is in the field of Ephron the Hittite, in the cave that is in the field of Machpelah, which is before Mamre, in the land of Canaan, which Abraham bought along with the field from Ephron the Hittite for a burial site. There they buried Abraham and his wife Sarah, there they buried Isaac and his wife Rebekah, and there I buried Leah–the field and the cave that is in it, purchased from the sons of Heth (Genesis 49:29-32).

At first glance it may seem insignificant or insensitive to focus on the place where one's body is to be buried. Jacob and his family were in Egypt, enjoying a successful situation there under the protection of Joseph. Why make the family take the long trip back to the land of Canaan with his body? More importantly, what does his grave site have to do with his legacy?

We have already noted how Jacob blessed his children and grandchildren (chapter 15). As the conduit for the covenant given to his grandfather Abraham, Jacob's official blessing was part of the legacy that he left his family. But his legacy included more than a family that would become a great nation. It also included a land which his descendants were to occupy. His dying request to be buried in the land promised in the covenant with Abraham was not just the desire to be with his relatives in death. It was a statement of confidence that his descendants would indeed possess the land. What God had promised was as good as done even though they could claim only a small burial site and the little plot Jacob purchased on the eastern border when he returned from Syria

At this final stage of his life, Jacob did what is demanded of great leaders–he relinquished his role as competent leader. Bruce Wilkinson observed that a leader is driven to competence but may be required to break this bond with competence in order to leave the legacy that is most important. If competence is one's primary core value, it may be difficult, if not impossible, to leave a legacy that truly matters.

When we examine the lives and careers of Joseph, Daniel or Esther, a remarkable truth emerges. Their spectacular careers were only *platforms and pathways* to their ultimate destinies and legacies. The plan was not for Esther to enjoy a Queen for a Day fantasy. She had to put her Cinderella queenship on the line to deliver her people.

Daniel's spectacular rise to power after being deported to Babylon was his platform to give us one of the greatest and most unique prophetic books in the Bible and be the voice of God to the highest strata of Babylonian society. To do so, he had to be willing to sacrifice his competency to potentially become a meal for lions.

Joseph did not become astoundingly successful as vice regent in Egypt for the ultimate "I told you so" to his brothers. On the contrary, he said clearly that he was not there for himself but to provide a place for those same brothers who sold him as a slave and for the nation that would emerge years later. If any of them had made their career or competence their first priority, they would have failed tragically.

I make this observation because of the competency pressure leaders face to survive or run ahead of the pack. It is startling to realize that we may need to break with our consuming drive for competence to reach the more important destination of convergence.

This is where Jacob was. His success in developing a great livestock venture was behind him. The only significance of his assets was their ability to help finance his family and insure their success in exile. Being a competent leader was no longer his concern–those days were past for him. His issue now was living into his final role and making a legacy statement for those who would come after him. Four hundred years later when his descendants struggled with leaving what had become their home in Egypt, they knew his body was already in the land that was their real home.

We can learn a lesson from Jacob. Don't be passive about what you think God wants to leave through you when you depart the earth. Dr. Ken Taylor developed the *Living Bible* for his children and eventually millions of copies were sold throughout the world. He planned his funeral two years before he died, and one of the special touches was the choir he requested. It was composed of fifty of his grandchildren and great grandchildren–part of the legacy statement of a man who devoted much of his life helping children and families grasp Scripture to find God.

Perhaps you are *sublimating spirituality for competence* because you are driven on the highway of competency to reach objectives you have not examined carefully. You may finally be required to move beyond *competence to convergence* by assuming whatever role is required to leave the legacy designated for you, even if it means giving up how you have identified yourself for the past thirty years as the man or woman in charge! Learning this lesson in our family which is well stocked with leaders has been important for me. A daughter who is a leader in her own right, with a national platform of speaking and writing, recently told me, "Dad, you are easier to be with these days."

Your legacy may not look or feel like Jacob's, but if you are following the plan for your life that includes similar elements or priorities that we have observed in Jacob's life, you have a legacy to leave behind, whether or not you have ever figured out what it is. Perhaps God will save it as a surprise for you!

### Arriving – Becoming the Person You Were Meant to Be

A year before Ken Taylor died, he wrote an article urging Christians to serve others with pure motives in the narrow time frame we have in this life. His plea was powerful because he lived what he preached. Yet, what set Dr. Taylor apart from many others was not simply that he was responsible for the *Living Bible* or that he started and ran a power-house Christian publishing company. As wonderful as these accomplishments are, what made him such a special man is that his life was fully developed with respect to God, others and himself. For exactly the same factors we noted in Jacob's life, he had reached an unusual level of convergence.

In the article, Dr. Taylor predicted "that not many would give his death more than a passing thought" (*Christianity Today*). He was wrong! At his funeral 1,000 people gathered at Wheaton College to celebrate his life. The service was even broadcast nationally.

Ken Taylor became who he could be as a person. When I conversed with him at a dinner a few years ago, his role as a world-renowned publisher didn't strike me nearly as important as the person he was–an elderly man who humbly radiated a godly maturity with sixty-five years of marriage, family and business behind him. He made millions from the *Living Bible* alone but refused to touch the money personally; instead he and his wife chose to live simply. As with

Jacob, what tied everything together and empowered all his life was a maturing journey with God. The *Christianity Today* article was right, "We see that God has done wonderful things through Taylor. But more than that, we rekindle a gratefulness that there are men like Ken Taylor. Heroes inspire hope that we can be better people than we are. Taylor, then, must be a hero" (p.27).

He was a hero, and so is everyone else who reaches convergence with respect to God, in what they contribute to others and in what they become personally. Perhaps this is why the Bible says, "Precious in the sight of the Lord is the death of His godly ones" (Psalm 116:15). It must be assumed that they have reached convergence!

Jacob took a lifetime to grow up and become what he was capable of becoming. God met him in an encounter designed just for him and eventually Jacob was forced to confront himself more deeply than he could have ever done when he was a deceiver with his father.

After surviving desperate circumstances in a 1914 expedition to Antarctica in which almost miraculously not a single man was lost, Earnest Shackleton concluded:

> In memories we were rich. We had pierced the
> veneer of outside things. We had suffered, starved,
> and triumphed, groveled yet grasped at glory, grown
> bigger in the bigness of the whole. We had seen God
> in his splendors, heard the text that nature renders.
> We had reached the naked soul of Man (p. 187).

Driven to the nakedness of his own soul at Peniel, Jacob came to a level of personhood that we still celebrate today. In so doing, he experienced what Augustine longed for when he prayed, "Grant, Lord, that I may know myself that I may know Thee."

The two final crescendo chapters of the Bible take us

beyond our present era to a prophetic, visual description of what the eternal state will be like. Of all characters to appear in this grand finale–it is Jacob!

And he carried me away in the Spirit to a great and high mountain, and showed me the holy city, Jerusalem, coming down out of heaven from God, having the glory of God. Her brilliance was like a very costly stone, as a stone of crystal-clear jasper. It had a great and high wall, with twelve gates, and at the gates twelve angels; and names were written on them, which are the names of *the twelve tribes of the sons of Israel.*

We find Jacob's new name here because Israel became the name of the nation developing from his descendants. His new identity and name was so significant that he lost it to the nation who took it and became the vehicle through which God has carried out His plan in human history. But even though Israel became the name of the Jewish nation, it was still the new name given by God to Jacob.

Revelation speaks of the *new name* to be given by Christ to those who have followed the call of God on their lives: "To the one who conquers I will give him a white stone, with a new name written on the stone that no one knows except the one who receives it" (2:17). The new name must have something to do with what will make our lives individually distinctive among all other human beings who ever lived. Apparently, when Jacob was given the name Israel, he got his new name in advance!

The significance of this was captured by Jennifer Woodruff when she wrote,

I am not who I was
>   when all I knew was shame.
>   *Nor yet who I will be*
>       *when I have learned my name. (Italics* mine)

This is what John, the Apostle who wrote the Book of Revelation, meant when he recorded the inspiring words, "What we will be has not yet appeared: but we know that when He appears we shall be like Him, because we shall see Him as He is" (1 John 3:2).

Our final significance is waiting to be discovered. Jacob went a long way toward discovering his deepest identity. He approached this reality in terms of a shepherd and his sheep.

> He [Jacob] blessed Joseph, and said, "The God before whom my fathers Abraham and Isaac walked, the God who has been my shepherd all my life to this day, the angel who has redeemed me from all evil . . ."(Genesis 48:15-16).

The most closely connected bond between an animal and a person in that day was that of shepherd and sheep. The implication is only too clear–God knew everything about Jacob and still loved him enough to take complete care of him. Jacob, as the sheep, found his identity in his Shepherd's gracious concern for him. I wonder if David got the idea for Psalm 23 from Jacob and expounded on what Jacob had come to know implicitly! A net result of what Jacob learned in his career as a leader was to follow his Shepherd like a sheep.

How Jacob died, with his apparent full measure of satisfaction, significance and fulfillment, is a good reference point for us today. He was at peace with everything he experienced, lost, or endured. He took off the masks, got rid of the persona, and embraced what was deepest and truest in his being. When we reach the point of convergence, we are free to see ourselves appropriately, not fully or totally but enough to understand that who we are is good in the sight of God, and that He has been our Shepherd in this lifetime process.

While Jacob's life is a journey marked off by its geography–Home, Syria, the Land and Egypt–the places of his life are symbolic of something more essential. Celtic Christians captured this reality with *peregrinatio*, "a word and concept that is found nowhere else in Christendom." It indicates that "the really significant journey is the interior journey. As Dag Hammarskjold said, 'The longest journey is the journey inward.'. . . So, *peregrinatio* presents us with the idea of the interior, inward journey which is undertaken for the love of God, or for the love of Christ, *pro amore Cristi*." (pp. 7-8)

**Completion – The End!**

By looking at the finale of Jacob's life, we have identified three indicators of convergence with respect to God, others and ourselves. We will have matured with respect to God, left our legacy or completed our task with respect to others, and grown up or become who we can be individually. While there are surely other signs of convergence, these three will always be a part of the equation as it was for Jacob.

The emphasis of this chapter (and book) is not that we detach from the impassioned, compelling adventure of leadership in whatever marketplace or arena we operate. The critical mass gained by looking at Jacob is that our life experience and career must be part of a bigger picture and help drive us to spiritual formation, life development and finally *convergence!* The journey must reach the point of becoming who we are and doing what we can do. God is the ultimate Author, Designer and Enabler of this kind of life. We need to stay the course and persevere until our conquest is completed with *CONVERGENCE!*

When Jacob finished charging his sons, he drew his feet into the bed and breathed his last, and was gathered to his people (Genesis 49:33).

One's pilgrimage is "a transformative journey to a sacred center full of hardships, darkness, and peril" (Cosineau). Jacob took this journey to a sacred center all the way through his beleaguered life! He arrived. My hope and prayer is that you will do the same.

THE LEADER'S JOURNEY . . .

> **Finding the way to live *now* so that you arrive where you should be *then* by persevering until you complete the tasks that belong to you uniquely while you grow with respect to God, develop personally and live into your truest identity**

Questions for group or personal reflection:

1. How would you define *convergence*?

2. To what extent are you pursuing a course of action that leads you where you most need to go? How does one go about living a life that will end in *convergence?*

3. Have you grasped the big picture from Jacob's life and how it applies to you?

4. Now that you have shared Jacob's life journey, how have you been impacted or challenged? How might the rest of your life be changed?

5. Do you have adequate support or people who can partner with you to help you find the best path in your life journey? Do you need to take time for personal discernment and discovery as your follow-up of traveling with Jacob from womb to tomb?

**Response**

Prayer that you will gain a convergent life that comes together profoundly with respect to God, others, and yourself.

# ACKNOWLEDGMENTS

**To those who intersected the Jacob project and helped make this book happen:**

To Carole Streeter, who pushed the project along over a long period of time and helped shape it.

To Jim Cofield, whose editing, writing and coaching skills were a must for the final product.

To Wolfgang Kitner and the Fellowship of Companies for Christ who helped me bring to business leaders what has been entrusted to me.

# BIBLIOGRAPHY

Bellman, Geoffrey M. *The Consultant's Calling–Bringing Who You Are to What You Do*. San Francisco: Jossey-Bass Publishers, 1990.

Caner, Ergun and Caner, Emir. *Unveiling Islam: An Insider's Look at Muslim Life and Beliefs*. Grand Rapids: Kregel Publications, 2002.

*Christianity Today*. Carol Stream, Ill.: August 2005.

Cohn, Joseph Hoffman. *I Have Loved Jacob*. New York: American Board of Missions to the Jews, Inc., 1948.

Cosineau, Phil. *The Art of Pilgrimage*. Berkeley: Conari Press, 1998.

Costello, Andrew. *Cries . . . but Silent*.

DePree, Max. *Leadership Jazz*. New York: Doubleday, 1992.

DeWaal, Esther. *The Celtic Way of Prayer*. London: Hodder & Stoughton, 1996.

*Daily Herald*. Section 1-14, 6/1/04; Section 4-1, 7/13/04; Section 4-1, 3/16/05.

Draper, Edythe. *Draper's Book of Quotations for the Christian World*. Wheaton, Ill.: Tyndale House, 1992.

Epp, Theodore H. *The God of Abraham, Isaac and Jacob*. Lincoln, Neb.: Back to the Bible, 1970.

Hart, Archibald D. *Unmasking Male Depression*. Nashville,

Tenn.: W Publishing Group, 2001.

Herbert, A.S. *Genesis 12-50*. London: SCM Press, Ltd., 1962.

Merton, Thomas. *The Inner Experience*. Cistercian Studies, 1983-85.

Issler, Klaus. *Wasting Time with God–A Christian Spirituality of Friendship with God*. Downers Grove, Ill.: InterVarsity Press, 2001.

Jones, W. Paul. *The Art of Spiritual Direction: Giving and Receiving Spiritual Guidance*. The Potters House Bookletter. Washington, D.C., Spring, 2004.

Judy, Dwight H. *Healing the Male Soul–Christianity and the Mythic Journey*. New York: Crossroads, 1992.

*Kindred Spirit*. Dallas Theological Seminary, Autumn 1999, V 23, # 3.

Leech, Kenneth. *Soul Friendship–Celtic Insights into Spiritual Mentoring*. London: Hodder & Stoughton, 1999.

Leupold, H.C. *Exposition of Genesis*. Grand Rapids: Baker Book House, 1942.

Lewis, C.S. *The Weight of Glory and Other Addresses*. Ed. Walter Hooper. New York: MacMillan Publishing Company, 1975.

Maloney, George. *Alone with the Alone*. Notre Dame, Ind.: Ave Maria Press, 1982.

Marshal, Michael. *Commentary on Psalm 40, 5. Flame in the Mind–A Journey of Spiritual Passion.* Grand Rapids: Zondervan, 2002.

McGwire, Mark. *USA Weekend.*

Merton, Thomas. *Dialogues with Silence*. San Francisco: Harper, 2001.

Meyer, F.B. *Israel: A Prince With God*. New York: Fleming H. Revell.

Mulholland Jr., M. Robert. *Invitation to a Journey: A Road Map for Spiritual Formation*. Downers Grove, Ill.:

InterVarsity Press, 1993.

Neander, Joachim. *Praise to the Lord, the Almighty,* 1680.

Mulholland, Robert. *Shaped by the Word: The Power of Scripture in Spiritual Formation.* Nashville, Tenn.: The Upper Room, 1985.

*The New Dictionary of Thoughts.* Comp by Tyron Edwards, etc. New York: Standard Book Company, 1959.

Palmer, Parker. *Let Your Life Speak: Listening for the Voice of Vocation.* San Francisco: Jossey-Bass, 2000.

*The Pocket Webster School and Office Dictionary.* New York: Pocket Books–Simon and Schuster, 1974.

Powell, John. *Why Am I Afraid to Tell You Who I Am.* Chicago: Argus Communications, 1969.

Rembrandt. *The New Dictionary of Thoughts.* p.159.

Rendall, T.S. Prairie Bible Institute Pamphlet Series, Three Hills, Alberta, 1965-69.

Rolheiser, Ronald. *Against an Infinite Horizon.* New York: Crossroads, 2001.

Sanford, John A. *The Man Who Wrestled with God–Light from the Old Testament on the Psychology of Individuation.* New York: Paulist Press, 1981.

Schaeffer, Franky. *Addicted to Mediocrity. 20$^{th}$ Century Christians and the Arts,* Westchester, Ill.: Crossway Books, 1981.

Simon, Alvah. *North to the Night–A Year in the Arctic Ice.* New York: McGraw-Hill, 1999, p. 311.

Simpson, Ray. *Exploring Celtic Spirituality.* London: Hodder and Stoughton, 1955.

*The Seasons of a Man's Life.* New York: Alfred A. Knopf, 1978.

Smalley, Gary and Trent, John. *The Gift of the Blessing.* Nashville: Thomas Nelson Publishers, 1993.

Tolkien, J.R.R. *The Return of the King.* New York: Ballantine Books, 1983.

Van Haitsma, John P. *The Supplanter Undeceived.* Grand

Rapids: Privately printed, 1941.

Warren, Rick. *The Purpose Driven Life–What on Earth Am I Here For?* Grand Rapids: Zondervan, 2002.

*Webster's New Universal Unabridged Dictionary.* Dorset and Baber–Simon and Schuster, 1983.

Wicks, Robert. *After 50, Spiritually Embracing Your Own Wisdom Years.* New York: Paulist Press, 1997.

Wilkinson, Bruce. *The Nine Steps from Conversion to Convergence.* Fellowship of Companies for Christ International. FCCI Master's Series.

Zusya, Rabbi Martin Buber. *Tales of the Hasidim: The Early Masters.* New York: Schocken Books, 1975.

Printed in the United States
39765LVS00003B/1-129